Read a Book—Make a Book
How to Make Books
with Children Series

Encourage your students to use the books they read as seeds to sprout new ideas and more books. In *Read a Book—Make a Book,* teachers and students read a book and then create a class or individual book in response.

The books featured cover a variety of topics and styles. There are picture books and chapter books, classics and just-released publications, fiction and nonfiction. Writing suggestions, step-by-step book-making directions, and patterns are all provided.

Use this book:

- As a literature sourcebook
  Read a Book-—Make a Book suggests books to read for specific topics.

- To extend storytime

- For cross-age projects
  Peer tutors and buddy classes will enjoy working on the book projects together.

- To create a classroom library
  Create dozens of different books for your classroom library featuring your own students as authors.

Authors: Jill Norris, Joy Evans
Illustrator: Cindy Davis
Editor: Marilyn Evans
Desktop: Cheryl Puckett

Evan-Moor
EDUCATIONAL PUBLISHERS
EMC 778

Table of Contents

Pop-Up Book Binding

Paper Cover: Pop-up books generate lots of student interest. Students love to read the stories again and again to share the excitement of seeing the pop-up revealed. Follow these steps for easy, successful binding:

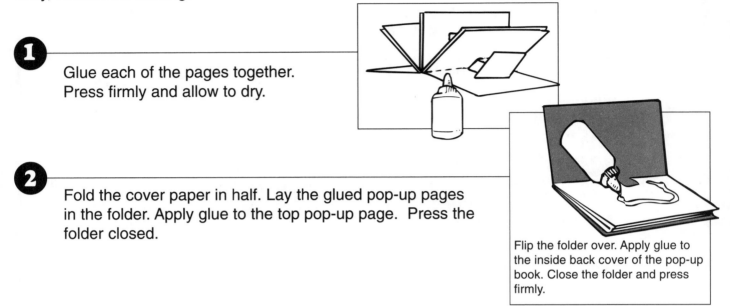

1 Glue each of the pages together. Press firmly and allow to dry.

2 Fold the cover paper in half. Lay the glued pop-up pages in the folder. Apply glue to the top pop-up page. Press the folder closed.

Flip the folder over. Apply glue to the inside back cover of the pop-up book. Close the folder and press firmly.

Cloth or Wallpaper Cover: Cardboard covered with cloth or wallpaper may be used to create sturdy and impressive covers for student pop-up books.

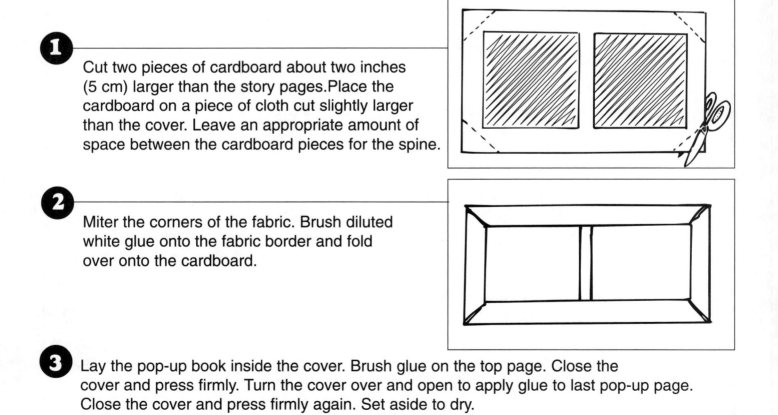

1 Cut two pieces of cardboard about two inches (5 cm) larger than the story pages. Place the cardboard on a piece of cloth cut slightly larger than the cover. Leave an appropriate amount of space between the cardboard pieces for the spine.

2 Miter the corners of the fabric. Brush diluted white glue onto the fabric border and fold over onto the cardboard.

3 Lay the pop-up book inside the cover. Brush glue on the top page. Close the cover and press firmly. Turn the cover over and open to apply glue to last pop-up page. Close the cover and press firmly again. Set aside to dry.

Hinged Binding

A hinged binding is appropriate if the book contains many pages and you want to use tagboard or another heavy material for the cover. The hinged book creates a book cover that opens easily and stands up to many readings.

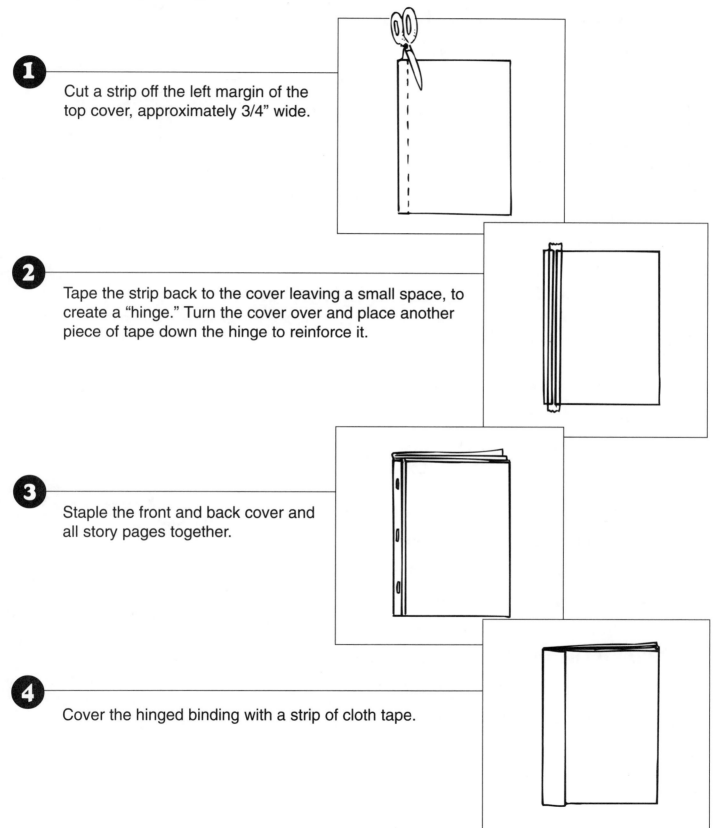

1 Cut a strip off the left margin of the top cover, approximately 3/4" wide.

2 Tape the strip back to the cover leaving a small space, to create a "hinge." Turn the cover over and place another piece of tape down the hinge to reinforce it.

3 Staple the front and back cover and all story pages together.

4 Cover the hinged binding with a strip of cloth tape.

I Unpacked My Grandmother's Trunk

by Susan Ramsey Hoguet; E. P. Dutton, 1983

Book Project

After You Read

Conduct a discussion about trunks to gather writing ideas.

• If you had a trunk what treasures would you put inside?

• Think about favorite book characters. What treasures would those characters put in their trunks?

Now Write!

• Tell about the treasures in your trunk; why are they special to you?

• Choose several items that your favorite character would store in a trunk. Why did you choose them?

Mommy gave me her dress shoes.
Daddy gave me his old shirt.
Gramps gave me a black hat.
Grandma gave me a long skirt.
I keep them in my dress-up trunk
With a shawl of purple and green.
I put them on and pretend
I'm going to visit the queen.

Jill Norris

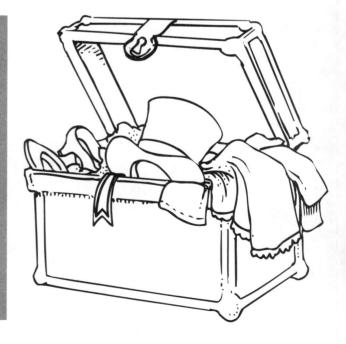

   Read a Book, Make a Book EMC 778

Make a Book...

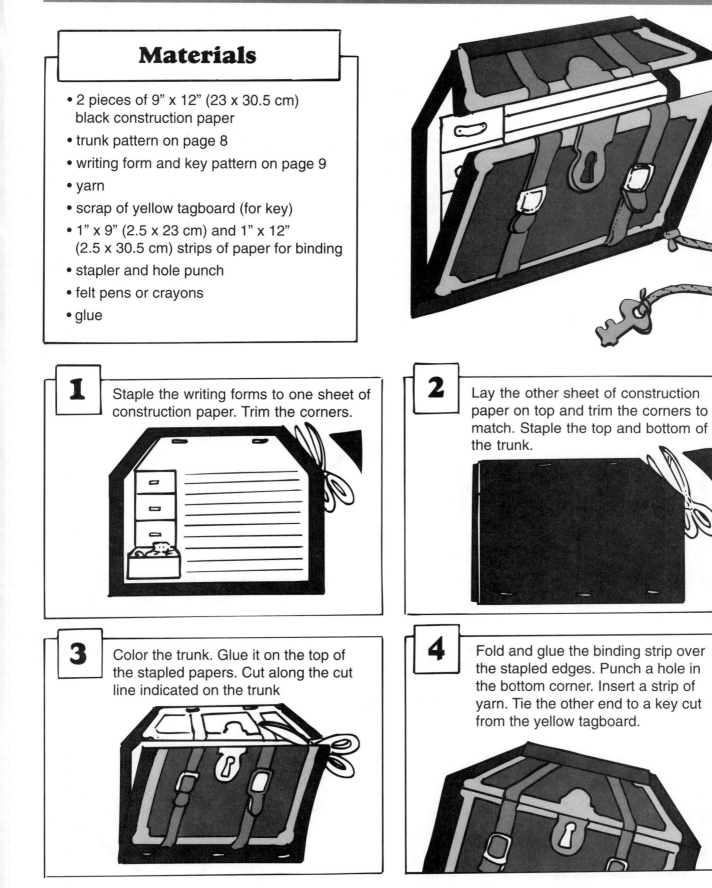

Materials

- 2 pieces of 9" x 12" (23 x 30.5 cm) black construction paper
- trunk pattern on page 8
- writing form and key pattern on page 9
- yarn
- scrap of yellow tagboard (for key)
- 1" x 9" (2.5 x 23 cm) and 1" x 12" (2.5 x 30.5 cm) strips of paper for binding
- stapler and hole punch
- felt pens or crayons
- glue

1 Staple the writing forms to one sheet of construction paper. Trim the corners.

2 Lay the other sheet of construction paper on top and trim the corners to match. Staple the top and bottom of the trunk.

3 Color the trunk. Glue it on the top of the stapled papers. Cut along the cut line indicated on the trunk

4 Fold and glue the binding strip over the stapled edges. Punch a hole in the bottom corner. Insert a strip of yarn. Tie the other end to a key cut from the yellow tagboard.

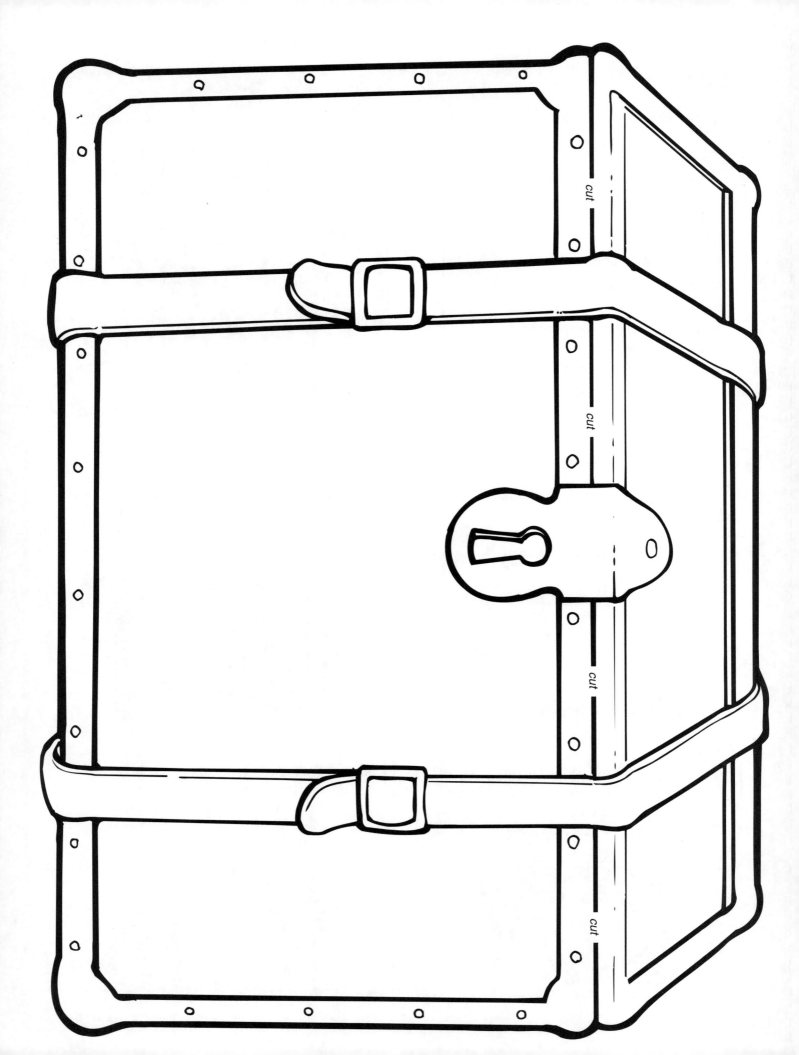

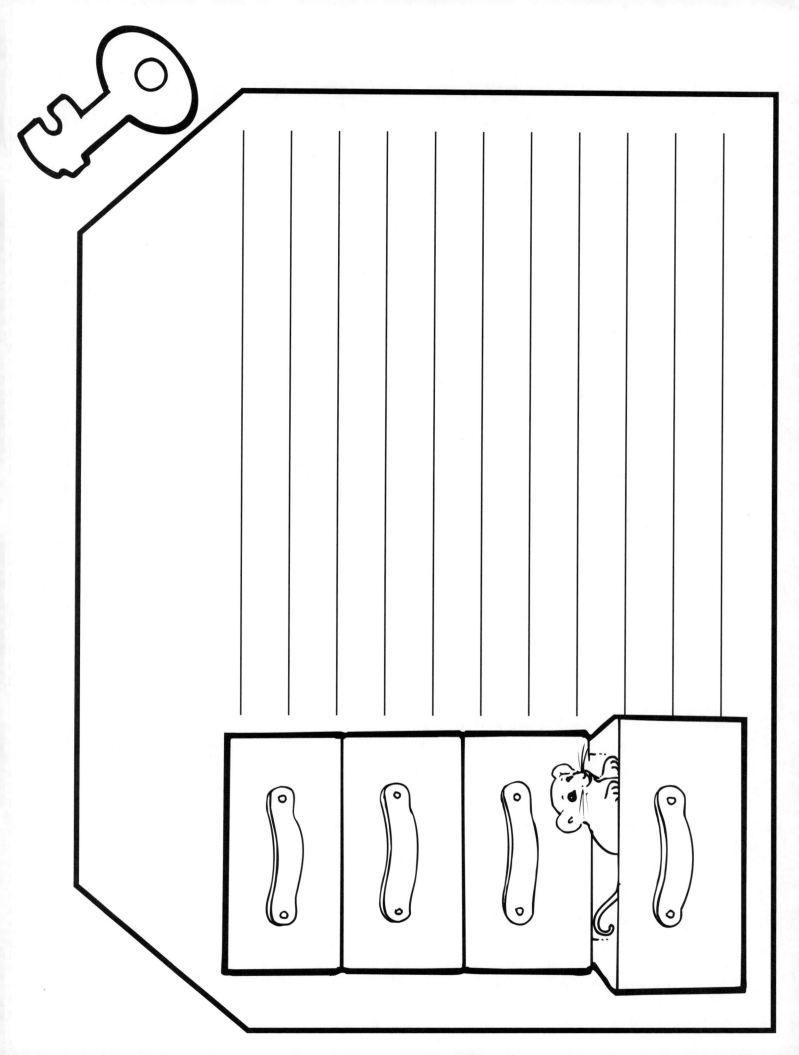

The Popcorn Book
by Tomie de Paola; Holiday House, 1978

Book Project

After You Read

You'll need:
- a large flat area near an electrical outlet
- a sheet
- an old-fashioned popcorn popper or a heavy kettle and a hot plate
- salad oil
- unpopped popcorn
- extension cord

1. Spread the sheet out. Students will sit around the edge as observers. (Warn students not to touch anything until you release them from their observer status.)

2. Place the popcorn popper in the center of the sheet.

3. Measure the oil and popcorn and add it to the popper.

4. Do **not** put on the top. Plug the popper in.

5. Use all your senses to observe what happens. Note all the changes that occur. (A volcano of popcorn will erupt from the popper.)

6. Talk about what you saw and then enjoy a yummy snack.

Now Write!

Describe the adventure of a kernel:
- from the kernel's point of view
- from a hungry watcher's point of view
- from an old maid's (unpopped kernel's) point of view

Tiny yellow kernels
Heated in the pot
Become puffy morsels...
I could eat a lot!

Jill Norris

Make a Book...

Popcorn Popper
Double-Hinged Book

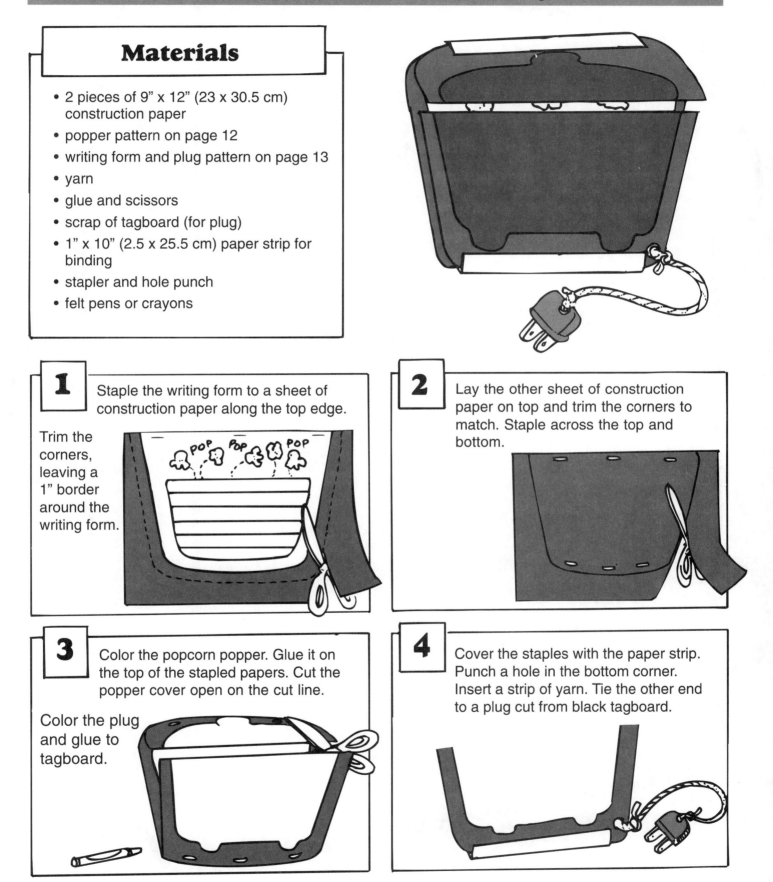

Materials

- 2 pieces of 9" x 12" (23 x 30.5 cm) construction paper
- popper pattern on page 12
- writing form and plug pattern on page 13
- yarn
- glue and scissors
- scrap of tagboard (for plug)
- 1" x 10" (2.5 x 25.5 cm) paper strip for binding
- stapler and hole punch
- felt pens or crayons

1 Staple the writing form to a sheet of construction paper along the top edge.

Trim the corners, leaving a 1" border around the writing form.

2 Lay the other sheet of construction paper on top and trim the corners to match. Staple across the top and bottom.

3 Color the popcorn popper. Glue it on the top of the stapled papers. Cut the popper cover open on the cut line.

Color the plug and glue to tagboard.

4 Cover the staples with the paper strip. Punch a hole in the bottom corner. Insert a strip of yarn. Tie the other end to a plug cut from black tagboard.

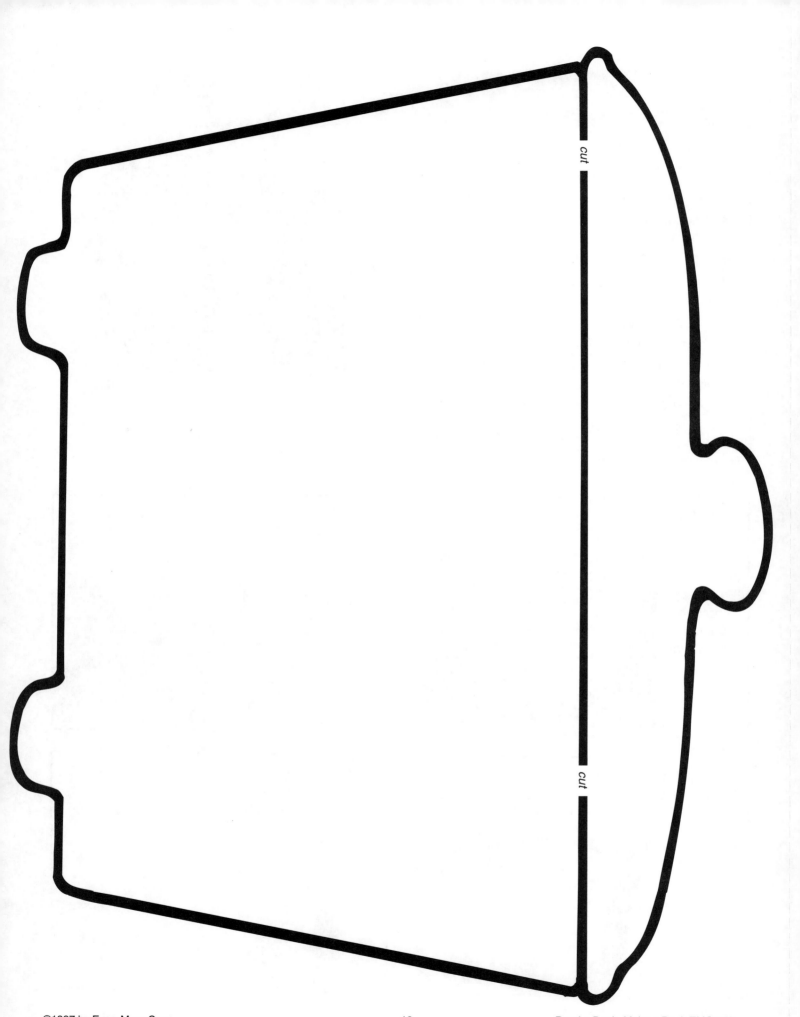

cut

cut

Read a Book, Make a Book EMC 778

Mr. Popper's Penguins

by Richard and Florence Atwater; Little, Brown, 1938

Book Project

After You Read

- Read additional nonfiction books about penguins to support the information presented in Mr. Popper's Penguins.

- Create a chart about the special characteristics of penguins.

- List penguin words in a word bank.

  words that tell how penguins move—waddle, slide

  words that tell how penguins eat—gulp, peck

  words that describe how penguins look—shiny, stiff

Now Write!

Use the information you gathered as the basis for writing about penguins.

- Pretend to be Dr._____, a scientist in Antarctica. Write about your observations of penguin behavior.

- Write a letter to Dr._____. Ask specific questions about penguins.

Mr. Popper's Penguins

Marching in a line.

Mr. Popper's Penguins,

A parade so fine.

Jill Norris

Make a Book...

Materials

- 12" x 18" (30.5 x 45.5 cm) light blue construction paper
- penguin forms on pages 16 and 17
- penguin baby patterns on page 17
- glue and scissors
- crayons or felt pens

1 Fold the construction paper into the center. Press down.

2 Round the top corners. Use a ruler to draw a line across the front 3" (7.5 cm) from top edge. Cut the front layer on that line.

3 Color the penguin. Glue the penguin on the inside layer. Staple together writing forms and glue back sheet to the penguin.

Optional: glue baby penguins on the flaps.

4 Decorate the front cover.

My Penguin Tale

Jane

Read a Book, Make a Book EMC 778

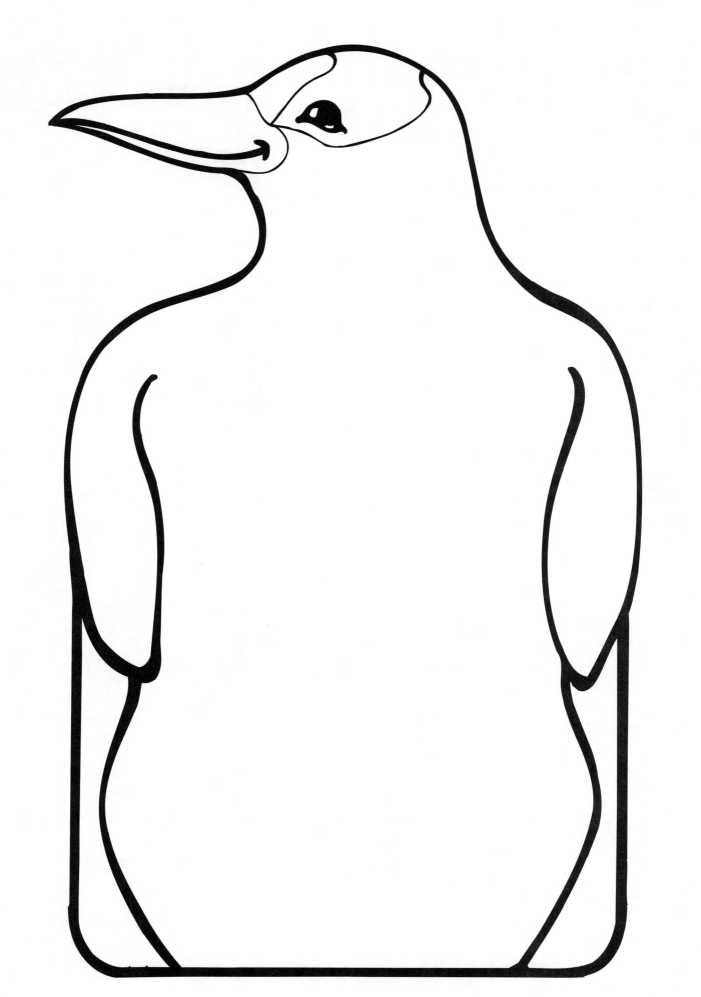

Read a Book, Make a Book EMC 778

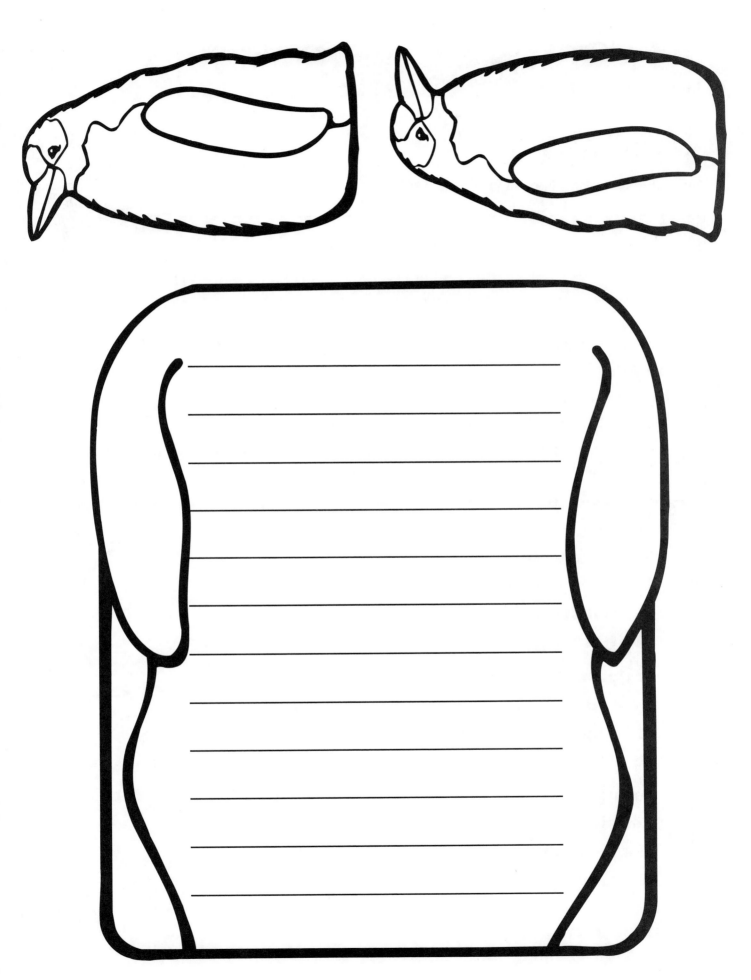

Read a Book, Make a Book EMC 778

Stellaluna

by Janell Cannon; Harcourt Brace, 1993

Book Project

After You Read

- Invite a "bat expert" to your classroom to talk about the special characteristics of bats.

- Turn out the lights and listen to a recording of night sounds.

Now Write!

Write about a night flight.

- What would it be like when everything was dark?

- Be sure to tell about the sounds and the smells around you, as well as the things that you see.

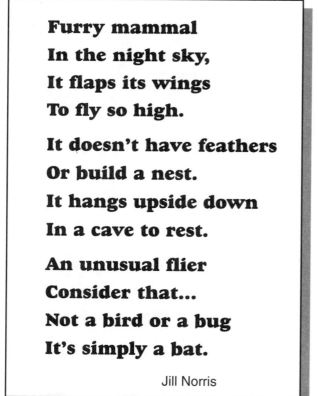

Furry mammal
In the night sky,
It flaps its wings
To fly so high.

It doesn't have feathers
Or build a nest.
It hangs upside down
In a cave to rest.

An unusual flier
Consider that...
Not a bird or a bug
It's simply a bat.

Jill Norris

Read a Book, Make a Book EMC 778

Make a Book...

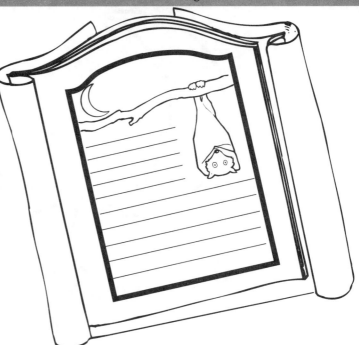

Materials

- two sheets of 9" x 12" (23 x 30.5 cm) dark blue construction paper
- bat and moon pattern on page 20
- writing form on page 21
- 1" x 9" (2.5 x 23 cm) strips of blue paper for binding
- stapler
- glue, scissors
- crayons or felt pens

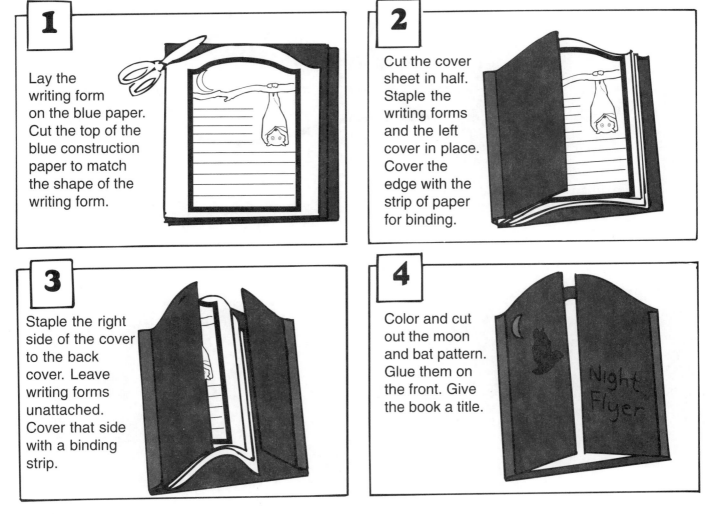

1
Lay the writing form on the blue paper. Cut the top of the blue construction paper to match the shape of the writing form.

2
Cut the cover sheet in half. Staple the writing forms and the left cover in place. Cover the edge with the strip of paper for binding.

3
Staple the right side of the cover to the back cover. Leave writing forms unattached. Cover that side with a binding strip.

4
Color and cut out the moon and bat pattern. Glue them on the front. Give the book a title.

Read a Book, Make a Book EMC 778

Read a Book, Make a Book EMC 778

How to Eat Fried Worms

by Thomas Rockwell; Franklin Watts, 1973

Book Project

After You Read

Tom and Alan and Joe spend some time arguing about the best place to dig worms. Where is the best place to dig worms?

- Discuss possible worm locations. Have each student choose a spot for surveying.
- Students should dig a shovel sample in their locations. (Remind them to get permission before digging.)
- Students then record the number and size of the worms that they find.

Now Write!

Write a report to summarize the results of the worm search: *The Best Place to Find Worms.*

It's hard for me to hold a worm

And feel it as it starts to squirm.

But it's harder still to bait the hook

When I go fishing at the brook.

Jill Norris

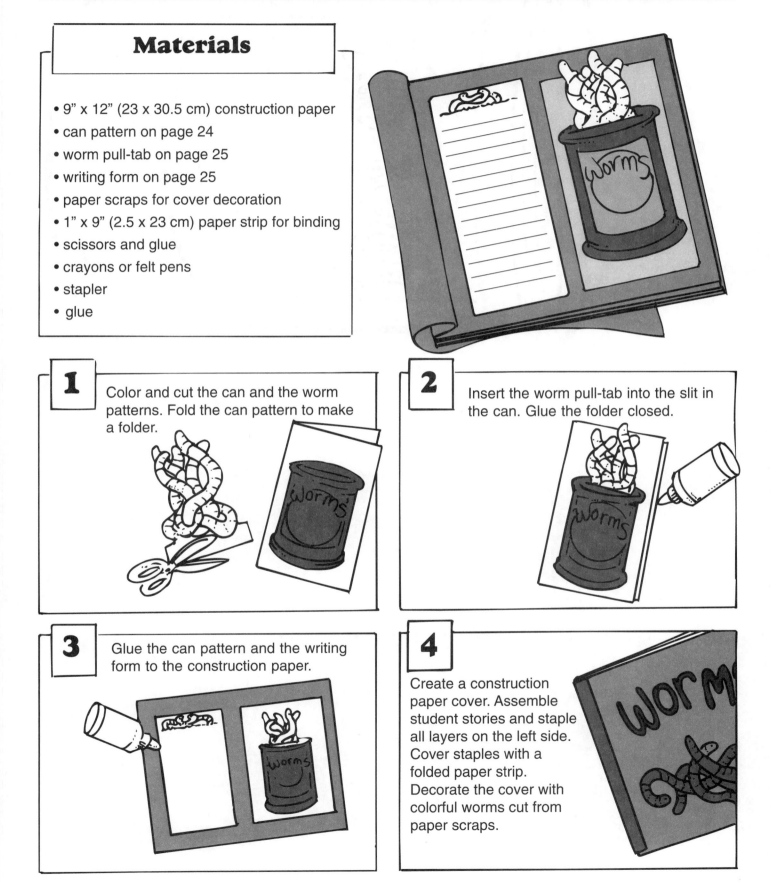

Materials

- 9" x 12" (23 x 30.5 cm) construction paper
- can pattern on page 24
- worm pull-tab on page 25
- writing form on page 25
- paper scraps for cover decoration
- 1" x 9" (2.5 x 23 cm) paper strip for binding
- scissors and glue
- crayons or felt pens
- stapler
- glue

1 Color and cut the can and the worm patterns. Fold the can pattern to make a folder.

2 Insert the worm pull-tab into the slit in the can. Glue the folder closed.

3 Glue the can pattern and the writing form to the construction paper.

4 Create a construction paper cover. Assemble student stories and staple all layers on the left side. Cover staples with a folded paper strip. Decorate the cover with colorful worms cut from paper scraps.

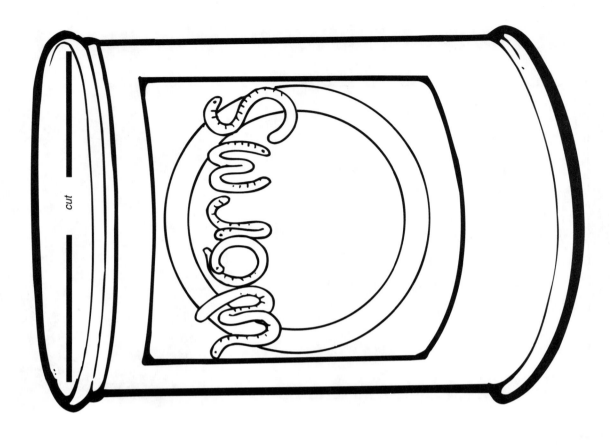

cut

fold

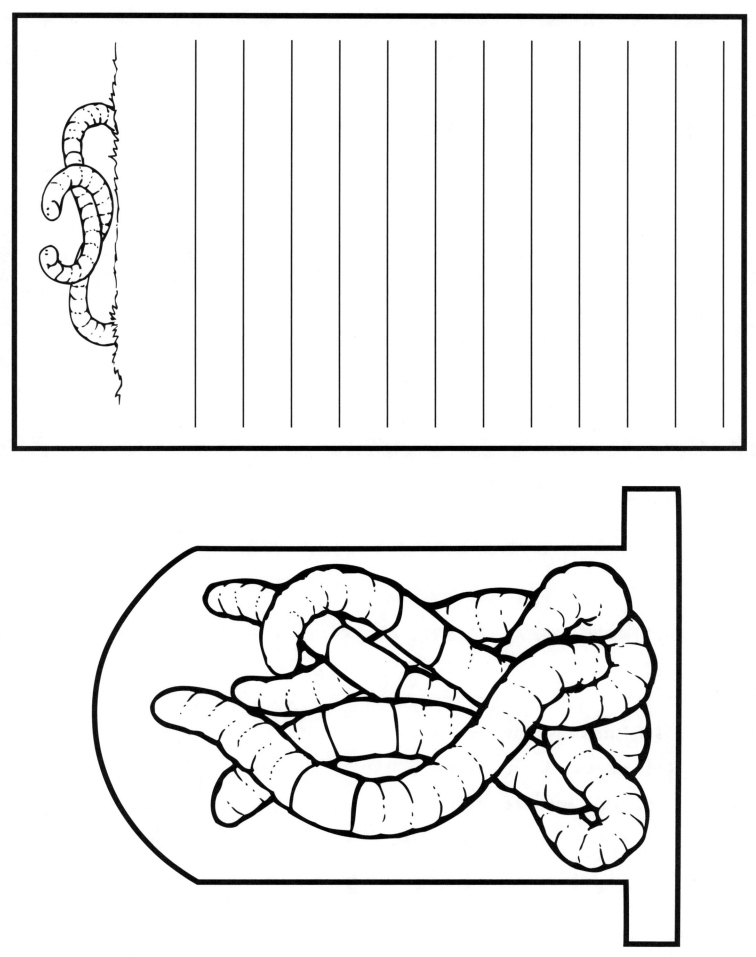

Read a Book, Make a Book EMC 778

A House for Hermit Crab

by Eric Carle; Picture Book Studio, 1987

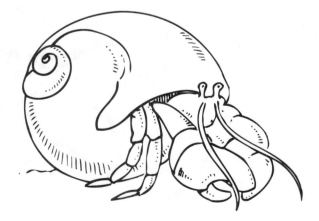

Book Project

After You Read

- If possible bring several hermit crabs into your classroom for observation. (Aquarium supply shops may carry them.) Pay particular attention to they way that they change shells.

- Discuss trying on shoes.

    How do shoes feel when they are too small?

    How do new shoes feel when you first put them on?

    What considerations make you choose one shoe over another?

Now Write!

Using their knowledge about trying on shoes, have students write a simple dialogue about a hermit crab who is searching for a new shell. Call the story "Trying on Shells for Size" or "If the Shell Fits."

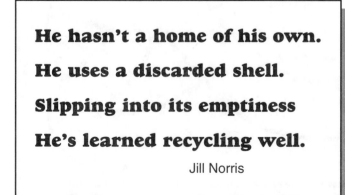

He hasn't a home of his own.

He uses a discarded shell.

Slipping into its emptiness

He's learned recycling well.

Jill Norris

Make a Book...

Materials

- 9" x 12" (23 x 30.5 cm) blue construction paper
- shell pattern on page 28
- crab pattern on page 29
- writing form on page 29
- paper scraps
- scissors
- hole punch
- yarn
- crayons or felt-pens
- glue

1 Color and cut the shell and crab patterns. Fold the shell to make a folder.

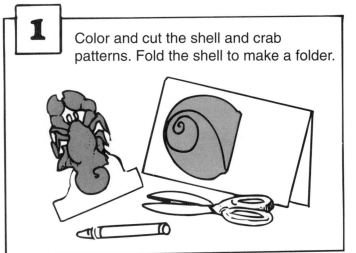

2 Insert the crab pull-tab into the slit in the shell. Glue the folder closed.

3 Glue the hermit crab pattern and the writing form to the construction paper.

4 Create a construction paper cover. Assemble student stories. Punch two holes through all the layers on the left side. Insert a piece of yarn and tie in a bow. Decorate the cover with seashells cut from paper scraps.

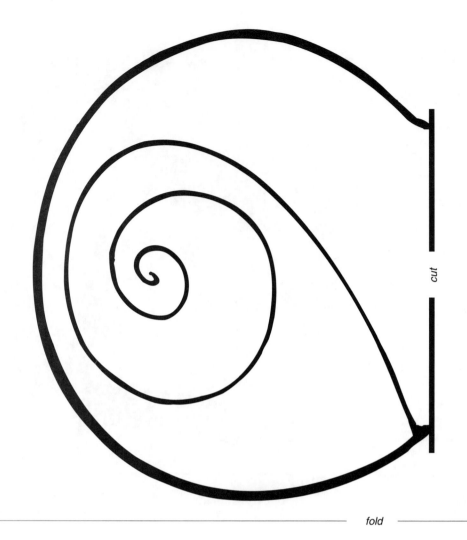

cut

fold

My Crayons Talk

by Patricia Hubbard; Henry Holt, 1996

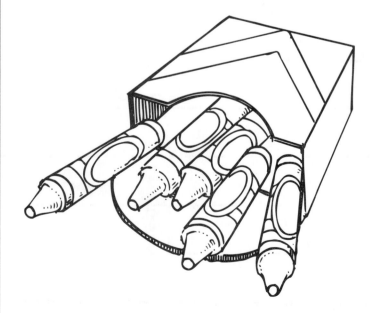

Book Project

After You Read

Imagine what the different colors in your crayon box might say and how they would say it.

- Choose a color.
- List the things that are that color.
- Think about different ways of saying things.
- Which ways are most like the color you are thinking about?

    Would a brown crayon mumble about dirt and melting chocolate?

    Would a yellow crayon sing of daffodils and sunbeams?

Now Write!

Use your ideas about colors and what they represent to write about a talking crayon.

**This is my crayon box.
Listen as it talks.**

> Red shouts.
> Green sings.
> Yellow laughs.
> Grey whispers.
> Black demands.
> White apologizes.
> Pink giggles.
> Blue sighs softly.

**This is my crayon box
Listen as it talks.**

Jill Norris

Materials

- 9" x 12" (23 x 30.5 cm) construction paper
- crayon box pattern on page 32
- writing form and pull-tab pattern on page 33
- scissors
- 1" x 9" (2.5 x 23 cm) paper strip for binding
- paper scraps to decorate the cover
- stapler
- glue

1 Color and cut the crayon box and pull-tab patterns. Fold the box to make a folder.

Color the stripes to match the crayons.

2 Cut the slit in the box pattern. Insert the pull-tab. Glue the edges of the folder closed carefully.

3 Glue the pull-tab folder and the writing form to the construction paper.

4 Add a construction paper cover. Staple all layers together on the left side. Cover the staples with a folded strip of paper.

Read a Book, Make a Book EMC 778

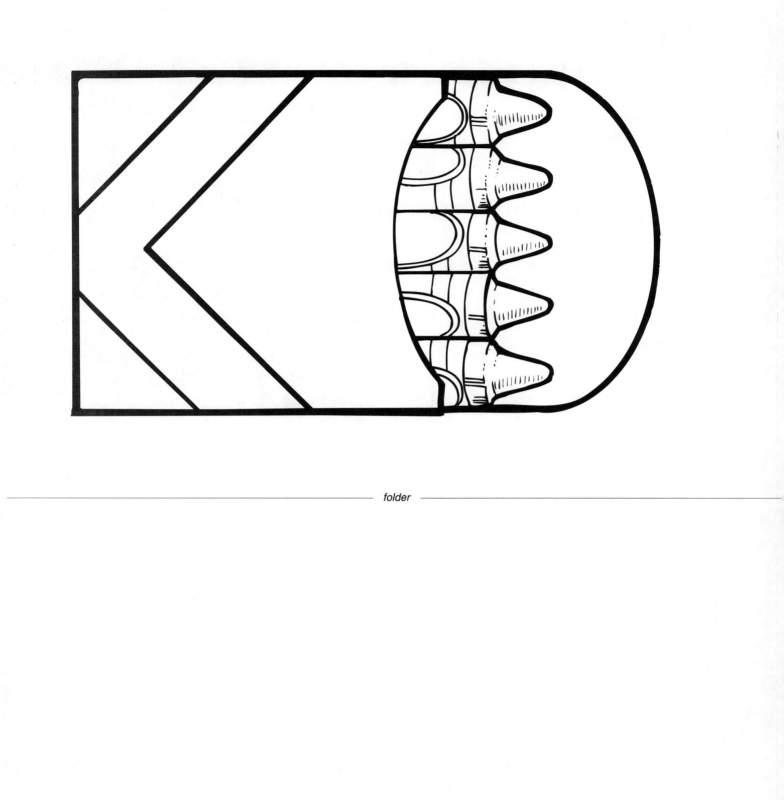

folder

32

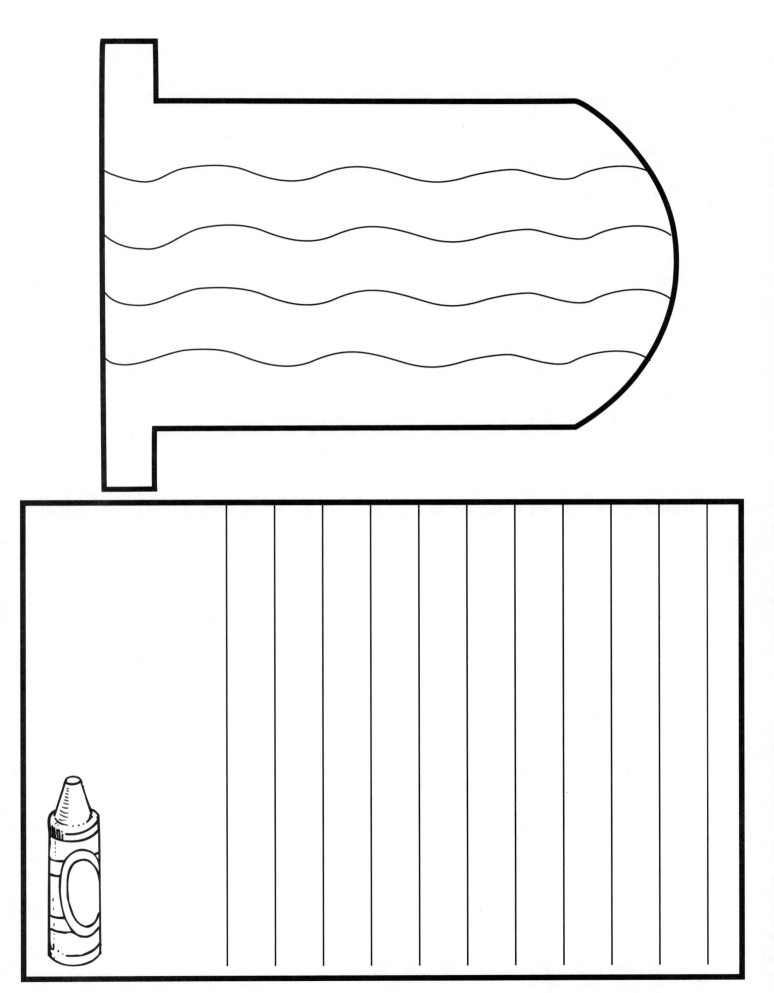

33

A Dinosaur Named After Me

by Bernard Most; Harcourt Brace and Company, 1991

Book Project

After You Read

Provide lots of reference materials so that students can find facts about their three favorite dinosaurs. (These can be chosen from the pictures provided on pages 36 and 37 or students can draw their own on the plain white paper.)

Now Write!

Write a paragraph about each of the three dinosaurs researched. Students should change the dinosaurs' names so that they contain the students' names as was done in Bernard Most's book.

Long, long ago
When the earth was new
Dinosaurs walked
And swam and flew.
Allosaurus,
Triceratops,
Apatosaurus, too.
Iguanodon,
Tyrannosaurus,
To name just a few.
Long, long ago
When the earth was new.
Huge dinosaurs lived
And small ones too.

Jo Ellen Moore

Make a Book...

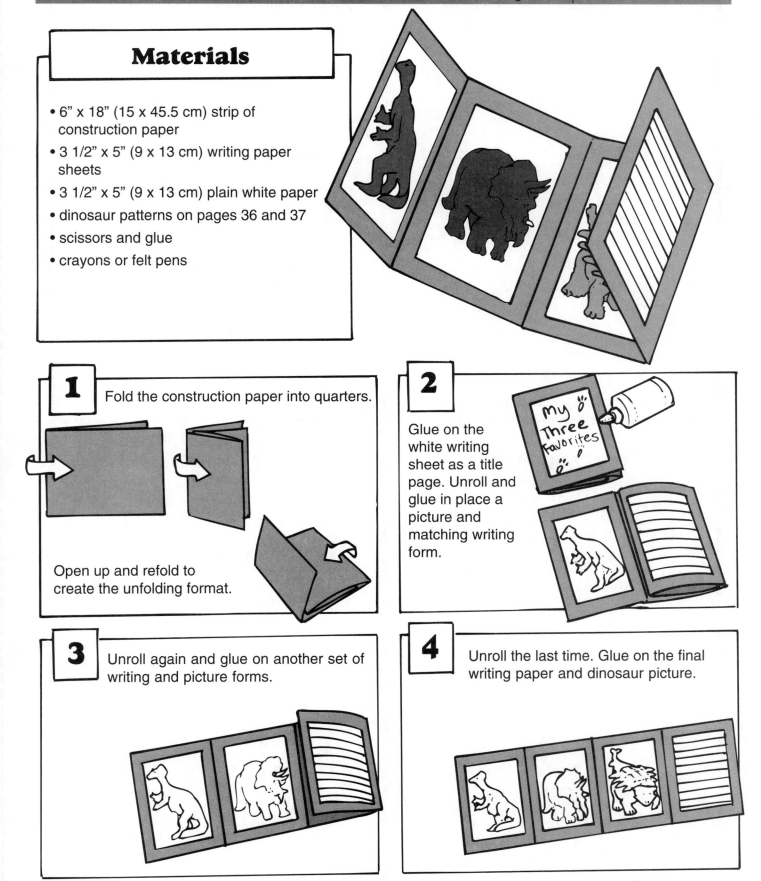

Materials

- 6" x 18" (15 x 45.5 cm) strip of construction paper
- 3 1/2" x 5" (9 x 13 cm) writing paper sheets
- 3 1/2" x 5" (9 x 13 cm) plain white paper
- dinosaur patterns on pages 36 and 37
- scissors and glue
- crayons or felt pens

1 Fold the construction paper into quarters.

Open up and refold to create the unfolding format.

2 Glue on the white writing sheet as a title page. Unroll and glue in place a picture and matching writing form.

My Three Favorites

3 Unroll again and glue on another set of writing and picture forms.

4 Unroll the last time. Glue on the final writing paper and dinosaur picture.

Read a Book, Make a Book EMC 778

Allosaurus

aka _____

Apatosaurus

aka _____

Brachiosaurus

aka _____

Stegosaurus

aka _____

Iguanodon

aka _____

Tricerotops

aka _____

Ankylosaurus

aka _____

Lambeosaurus

aka _____

The Little Engine That Could

retold by Watty Piper; Platt & Monk, 1990

Book Project

After You Read

1. Act out the story of the little engine.

- Have students ad-lib the lines or you paraphrase as they move through the story.

- Note the kindness and determination of the very little blue engine.

2. Discuss problems that your students have solved through determination. Perhaps there has been class problem that needs persistant work before it will be solved.

Now Write!

Write to tell how the problem was or will be solved. Be sure to use the words:
I think I can, I think I can…I thought I could, I thought I could.

Two engines at the front,

A line of cars in tow,

The train goes zipping by.

Where do you think it will go?

Jill Norris

Sky in a blur,

Shapes moving by,

The track's click clack ---

A lullaby.

Jill Norris

Make a Book...

Materials

- 9" x 12" (23 x 30.5 cm) construction paper
- train patterns on page 40
- writing form on page 41
- *I think I can* banner on page 40
- track patterns for the cover on page 41
- cellophane tape
- scissors and glue
- hole punch
- 3 metal rings
- crayons or felt pens

1 Cut out and color the train pattern. Tape the two sections together. Fold it back and forth in accordion fashion.

2 Color and cut out the banner and the writing form.

3 Glue the cut out parts to the construction paper. The train will *pull out* if only the last two sections are glued down.

4 Add a front cover and decorate with the track patterns provided. Punch holes along the left side and bind the book together with metal rings.

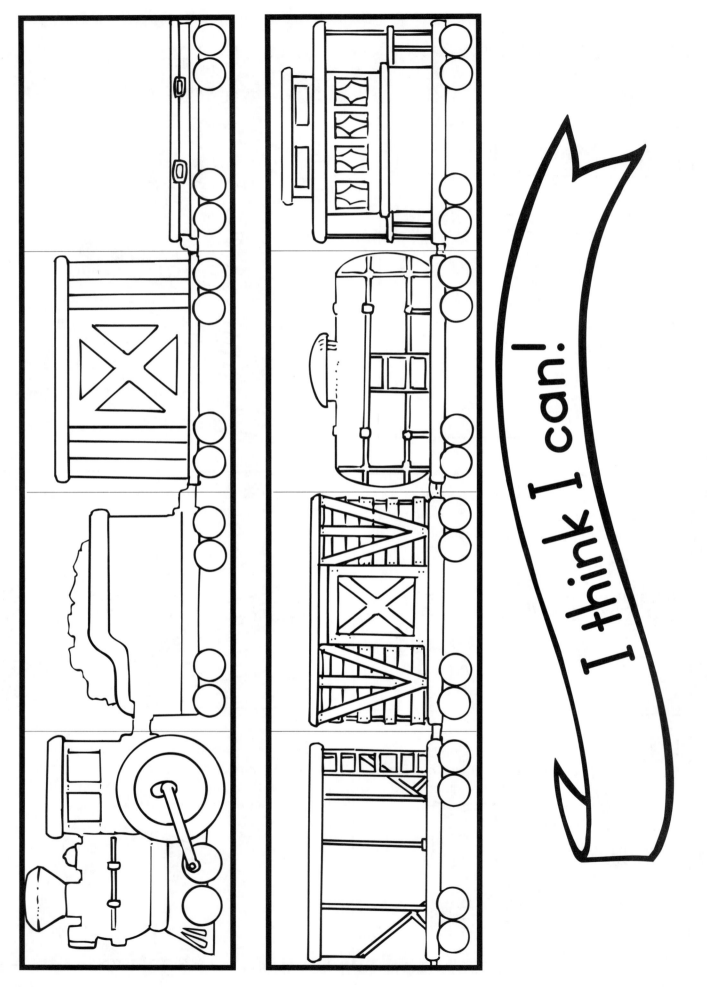

I think I can.

The Ant and the Elephant

by Bill Peet; Houghton Mifflin, 1972

Book Project

After You Read

List all the animals that Elephant helped. Tell what Elephant did for each animal.

Now Write!

Write a new version of **The Ant and the Elephant** using different animals and different problems.

Hint: List the animals and the problems first before beginning to write.
      Have a small animal save the day by helping the large animal at the ending.

Solid,

    Heavy,

        Sturdy,

           Slow...

              An elephant is strong, you know.

Jill Norris

Make a Book...

Materials

- patterns on pages 44 and 45
- scissors
- crayons or felt pens
- 9" x 12" (23 x 30.5 cm) construction paper
- 1" x12" (2.5 x 30.5 cm) paper strips for binding
- stapler
- glue

1 Color, cut, and fold the elephant and ant pattern.

2 Glue the pictures and writing form to the construction paper.

3 Lift up the flaps and write the moral of the story inside the folder.

4 Glue cover picture to a sheet of construction paper. Collect student stories and staple on the left side.

Glue on the paper binding strip.

Elephant Helps

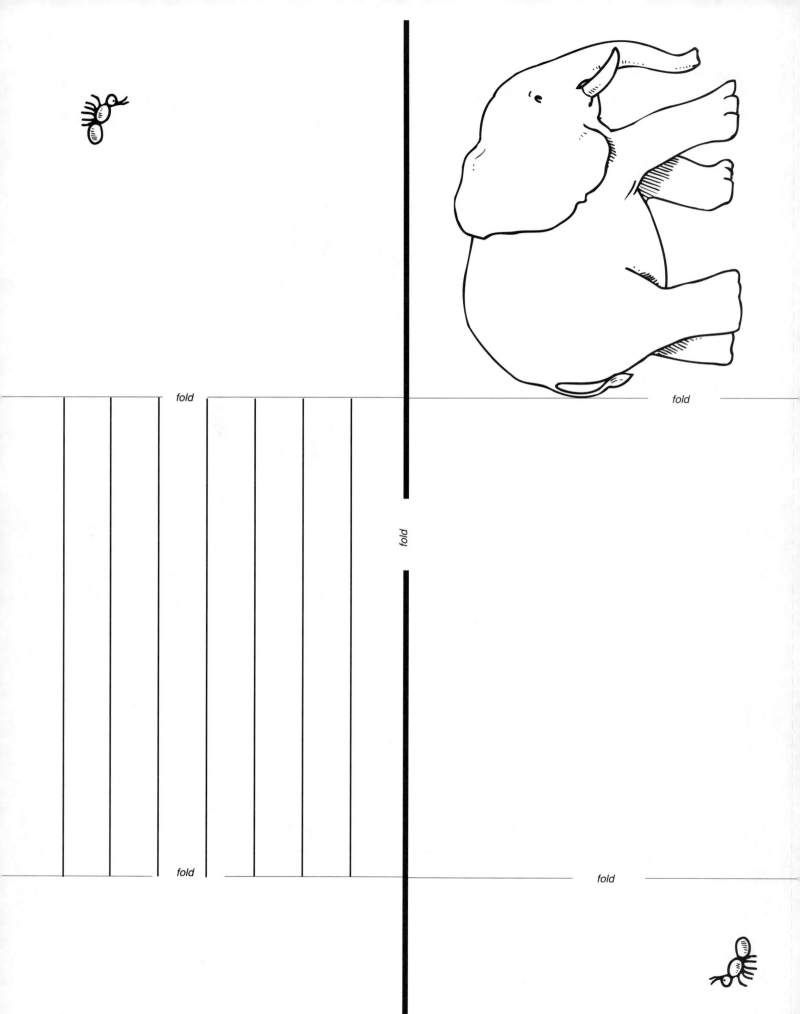

fold

fold

fold

fold

fold

Read a Book, Make a Book EMC 778

The Enormous Turnip

illustrated by Kathy Parkinson; Albert Whitman, 1986

The Turnip

by Walter de la Mare; David R. Godine, 1992

The Turnip: An Old Russian Folktale

illustrated by Pierr Morgan; Philomel Books, 1990

Above are three versions of the old folktale about the giant turnip.

Book Project

After You Read

Compare the versions of the turnip tale. Note the differences and the similarities.

Now Write!

- Write to retell the tale in your own way.
- Compare your version to the others.

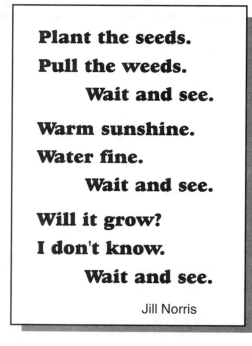

Plant the seeds.
Pull the weeds.
    Wait and see.

Warm sunshine.
Water fine.
    Wait and see.

Will it grow?
I don't know.
    Wait and see.

Jill Norris

Make a Book...

Materials

- 9" x 12" (23 x 30.5 cm) brown construction paper
- turnip pattern on page 48
- writing form on page 49
- title form on page 49
- scissors and glue
- hole punch
- twine
- crayons or felt pens

1 Color, cut out and fold the turnip pattern.

2 Glue the writing form and the folded turnip pattern on the construction paper.

3 Draw a horizon line to match up with the soil line on the folded turnip pattern. Add other details to the picture.

Color the lower sections of the pull-up brown.

4 Bind all stories together. Punch holes on the left side and secure with knotted twine. Glue the title form to the cover.

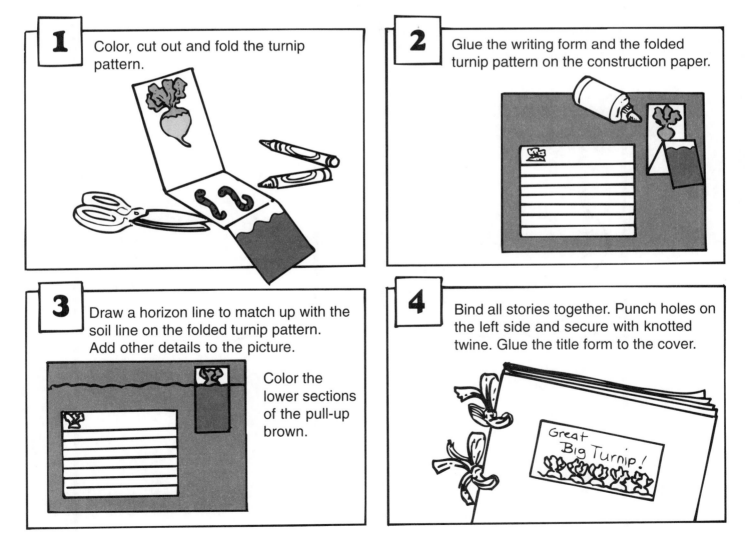

Read a Book, Make a Book EMC 778

fold

fold

fold

fold

The BFG
by Roald Dahl; Farrar, Straus, Giroux, 1982

Book Project

After You Read

The Big Friendly Giant is looking for a job.

1. List the special traits that would make him a valuable employee.

2. Think of jobs that would make good use of these talents and traits.

Now Write!

Write a resume for the BFG. Older students might also respond to the resume as potential employers. They could write a letter to the BFG offering employment or telling him to look elsewhere.

Big hands,

Big head,

Big ears...G - i - a - n - t

Big eyes,

Big smiles,

Big tears...G - i - a - n - t

Big arms,

Big legs,

Big toes...G - i - a - n - t

Big thumbs,

Big feet,

Big nose...G - i - a - n - t

Jill Norris

Read a Book, Make a Book EMC 778

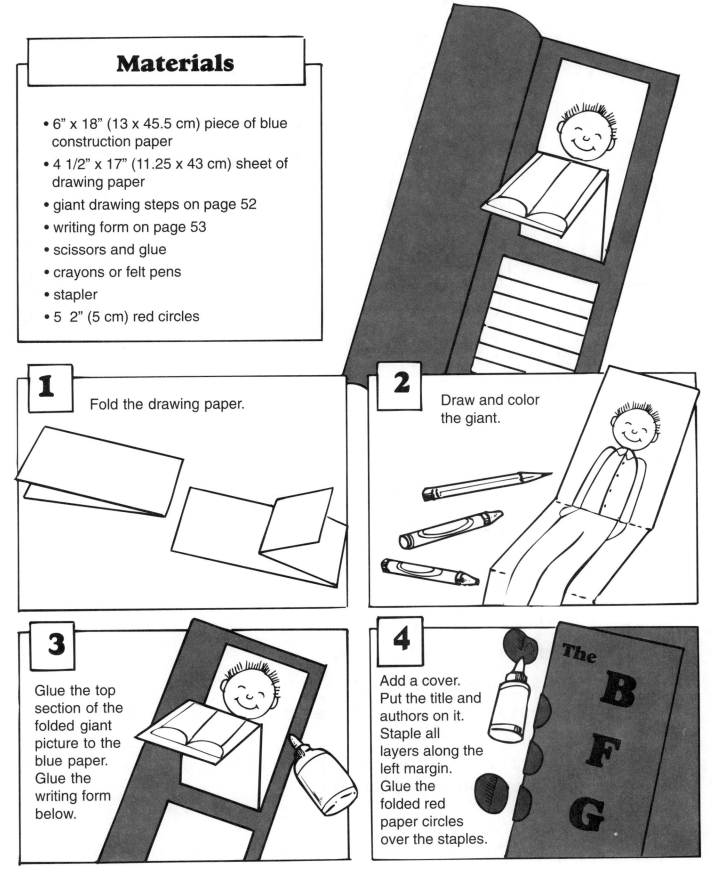

Materials

- 6" x 18" (13 x 45.5 cm) piece of blue construction paper
- 4 1/2" x 17" (11.25 x 43 cm) sheet of drawing paper
- giant drawing steps on page 52
- writing form on page 53
- scissors and glue
- crayons or felt pens
- stapler
- 5 2" (5 cm) red circles

1 Fold the drawing paper.

2 Draw and color the giant.

3 Glue the top section of the folded giant picture to the blue paper. Glue the writing form below.

4 Add a cover. Put the title and authors on it. Staple all layers along the left margin. Glue the folded red paper circles over the staples.

The B F G

Read a Book, Make a Book EMC 778

Giant Drawing Steps

1

2
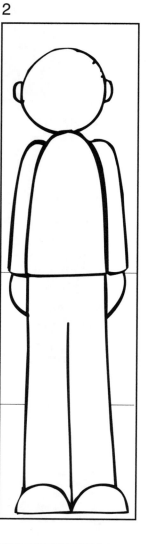

3
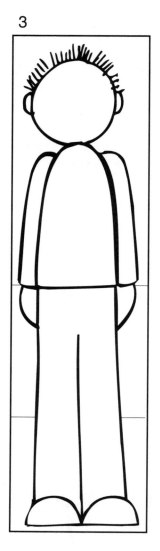

4
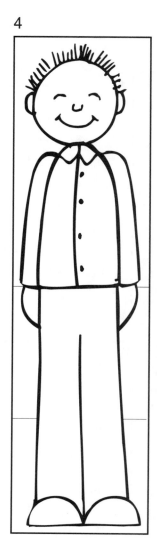

Add-Ons:

- Make a girl giant.

- Dress the giant for a party.

- Draw a pet for the giant.

- Make a backpack for the giant and fill it with giant-sized books.

- What would a giant eat for lunch? Fill a lunch box with an appropriate foods.

The

B F G

by

Pinocchio

by Chris McEwan; Doubleday, 1990

Book Project

After You Read

1. Describe different noses. This prewriting phase might include drawing as well as brainstorming.

2. List ways that noses might change. They might:

change color	shrink
grow	light up
flash on and off	

Now Write!

Write a tale about a character whose nose changes when the character lies.

The nose...grows.

Jill Norris

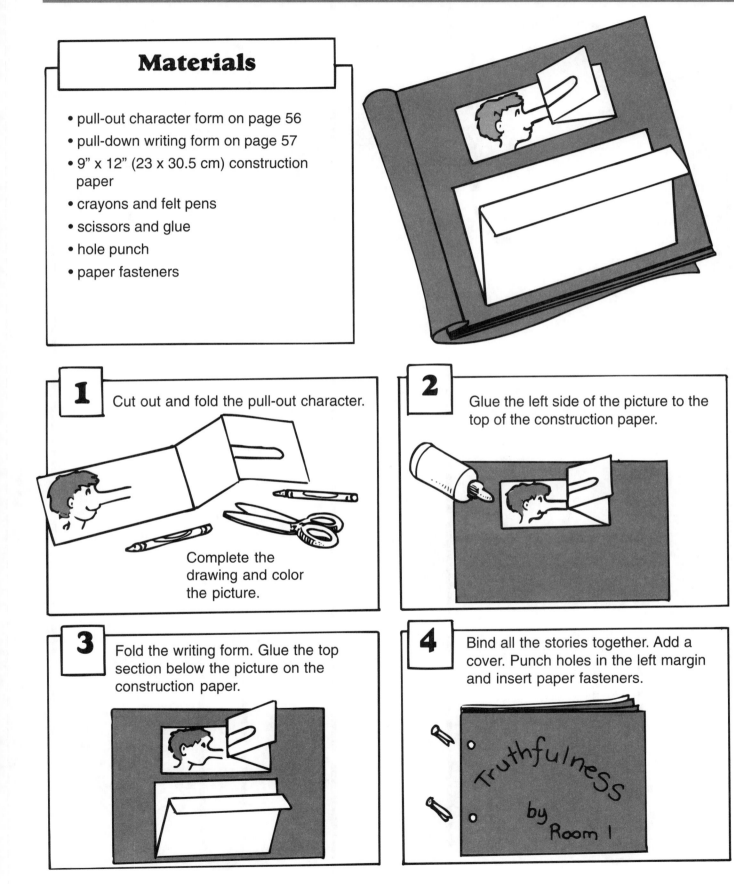

Materials

- pull-out character form on page 56
- pull-down writing form on page 57
- 9" x 12" (23 x 30.5 cm) construction paper
- crayons and felt pens
- scissors and glue
- hole punch
- paper fasteners

1 Cut out and fold the pull-out character.

Complete the drawing and color the picture.

2 Glue the left side of the picture to the top of the construction paper.

3 Fold the writing form. Glue the top section below the picture on the construction paper.

4 Bind all the stories together. Add a cover. Punch holes in the left margin and insert paper fasteners.

Truthfulness by Room 1

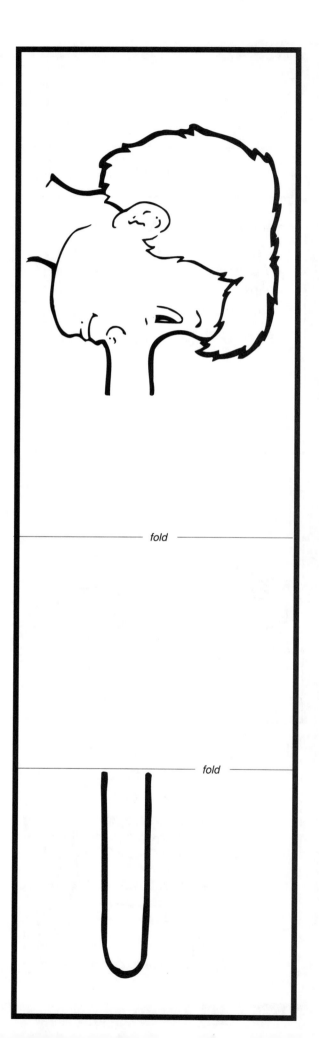

name:

title:

fold

fold

A Puppy Is Born
by Heiderose and Andreas Fischer-Nagel; G. P. Putnam's Sons, 1983

Book Project

After You Read

Discuss the special problems of a dachshund.

- tummy muddy on rainy days
- wide turns around trees and bushes
- hard to clean back legs
- can't see over a crowd

Now Write!

Write a story to tell how a dachshund overcomes one of these special problems.

Tiny legs close to the ground,

Pointed nose and tummy round,

My puppy's longer than he's tall.

But he doesn't seem to mind at all.

He happily plays and eats his food

Unaware that he lacks altitude.

Jill Norris

Make a Book...

Materials

- pull-out dog form on page 60
- rug writing form on page 61
- 9" x 12" (23 x 30.5 cm) construction paper
- 6 1/2" x3" (16.5 x 7.5 cm) writing paper
- scissors and glue
- crayons or felt pens
- hole punch
- yarn
- dog bones

1 Color, cut out, and fold the dog pattern.

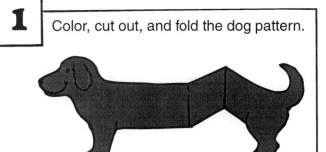

2 Cut out the writing form. Staple writing papers to the "rug." After the story is completed, glue the form to the construction paper.

3 Glue only the front part of the dog to the rug.

4 Assemble all stories together and add a cover. Punch two holes in the left margin and secure with yarn. Tie a bow in the yarn and tie dog biscuits to the yarn ends.

Watch Him Grow

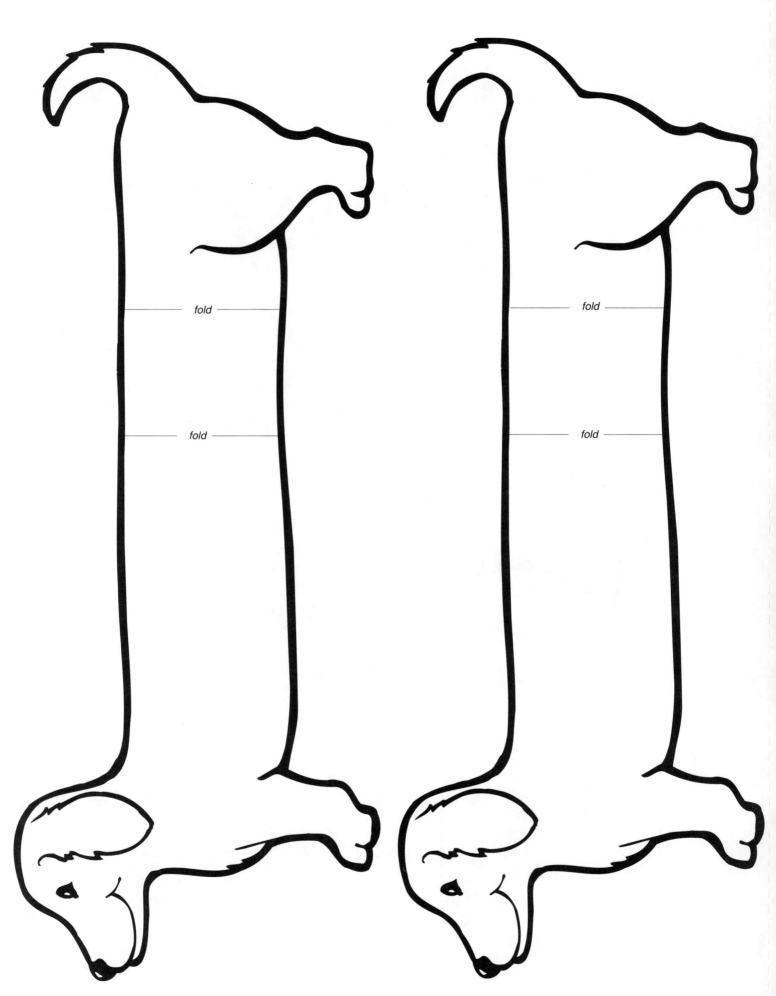

fold

fold

fold

fold

Read a Book, Make a Book EMC 778

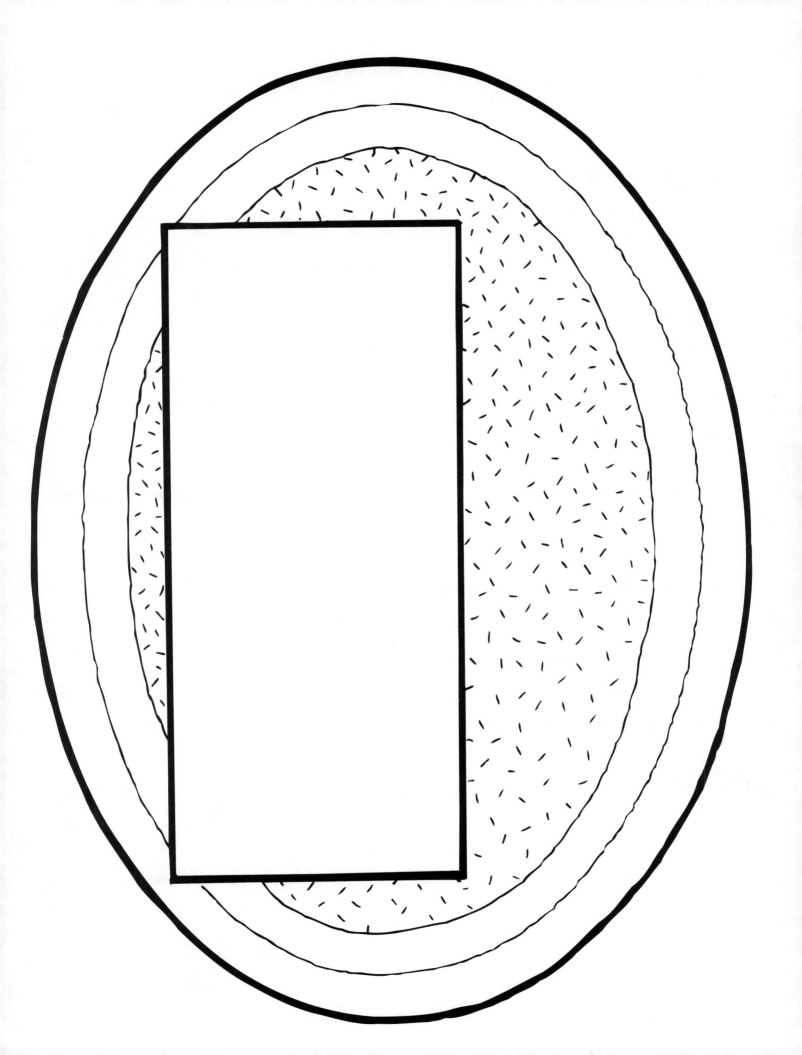

Cars and How They Go

by Joanna Cole; Crowell, 1983

Book Project

After You Read

1. Examine a real car. Locate the parts described in the book.

2. Invite a mechanic to talk about how the parts of a car work together.

3. Draw a car and label the parts.

Now Write!

Write about how a car works.

Pistons, radiator, fan belt, too.

Battery, spark plugs, what will I do?

My car won't start.

I must depart.

Could you help me, please? Thank you.

Jill Norris

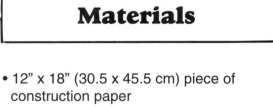

Materials

- 12" x 18" (30.5 x 45.5 cm) piece of construction paper
- car patterns on pages 64-66
- writing form on page 67
- scissors and glue
- crayons or felt pens
- stapler
- hole punch
- 3 sets of nuts and bolts

1 Color, cut out, and assemble the three layers of the car.

2 Staple the car layers together on the left side.

3 Cut out the writing form and glue it to the construction paper. Glue the car above.

4 Collect student stories and add a cover. Punch three holes along the left margin.

Secure the pages with nuts and bolts.

How It Works

car — top layer

Read a Book, Make a Book EMC 778

car — layer 2

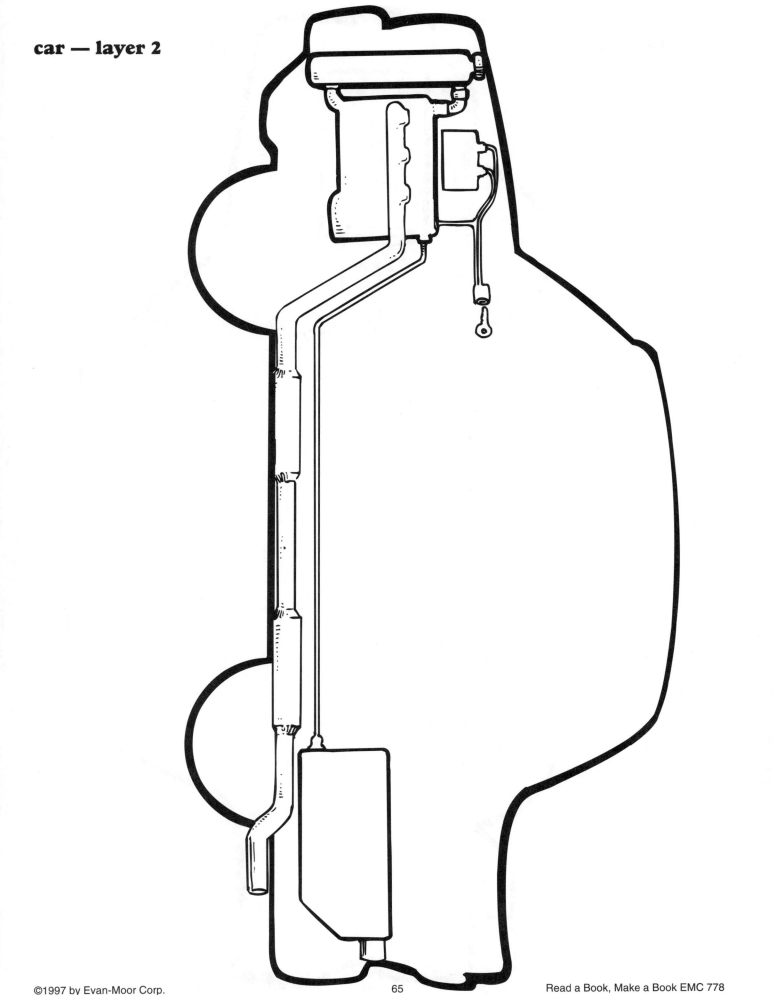

Read a Book, Make a Book EMC 778

car — layer 3

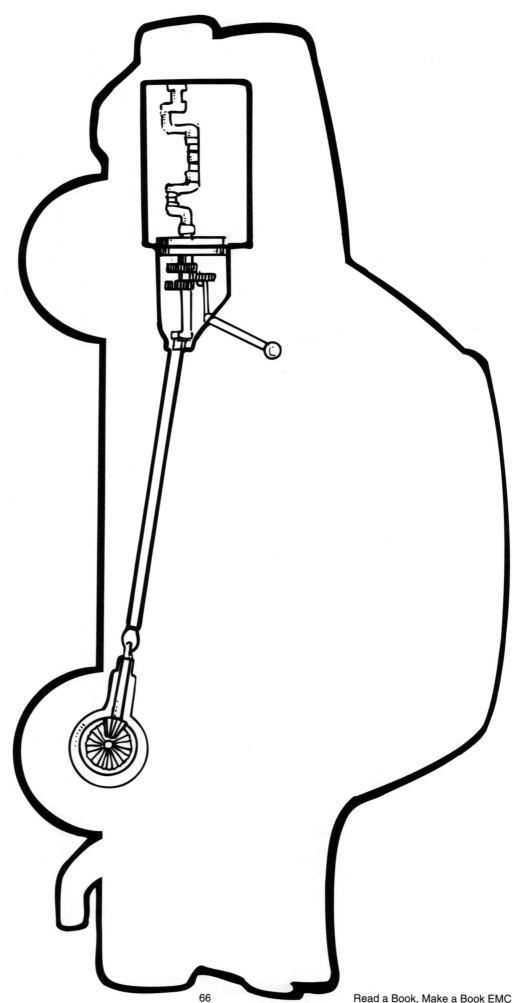

1

2

3

Have You Seen My Duckling?

by Nancy Tafuri; Greenwillow Books, 1984

Book Project

After You Read

Baby Duck had quite an adventure while Mother Duck searched for it. Have students imagine that they are the Baby Duck who had wandered away.

- What did you do?
- How did you feel?
- Did you learn anything?
- Would you wander away again?

Now Write!

Write about what the duckling would tell its mother when it was found.

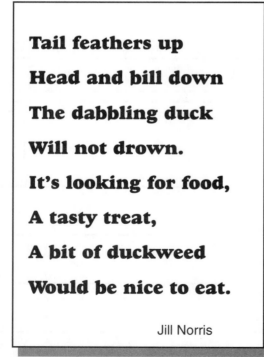

Tail feathers up

Head and bill down

The dabbling duck

Will not drown.

It's looking for food,

A tasty treat,

A bit of duckweed

Would be nice to eat.

Jill Norris

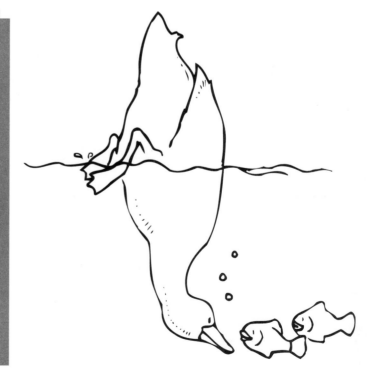

Read a Book, Make a Book EMC 778

Materials

- pond pattern on page 70
- duck and fish patterns on page 71
- student writing paper
- blue 9" x 12" (23 x 30.5 cm) construction paper
- green 9" x 12" (23 x 30.5 cm) construction paper
- scissors and glue
- crayons and felt pens
- stapler
- paper fastener

1 Color and cut out the patterns. Cut the slit in the river pattern.

2 Slip the duck in the slit and attach the duck to the water with a paper fastener. Duck can now dabble.

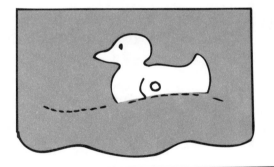

3 Cut the blue construction paper as shown. Cut writing paper in this same shape. Glue on the fish.

4 Fold down a strip of the green construction paper. Insert the pond, blue paper and writing paper in the fold and staple.

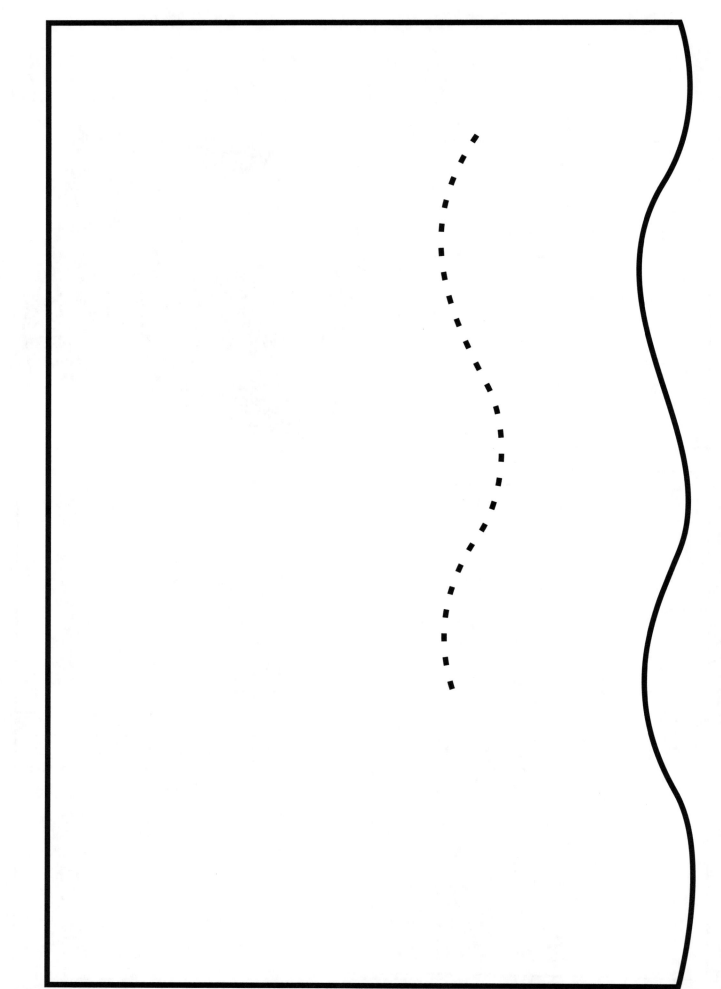

Read a Book, Make a Book EMC 778

71

Ant Cities

by Arthur Dorros; Crowell, 1987

Book Project

After You Read

1. Do step one of the book-making activity as a class. Discuss what you learned in **Ant Cities** and label the ants in your ant hill. Tell their names and the jobs that they do.

Now Write!

Write two short stories about life in an ant city.

- One story should be told from the point of view of an ant living inside the city.

- One story should be told from the point of view of a human watching the ant city from the outside.

In single file
They march along,
Amazing ants
Tiny, but strong.

Jill Norris

Make a Book...

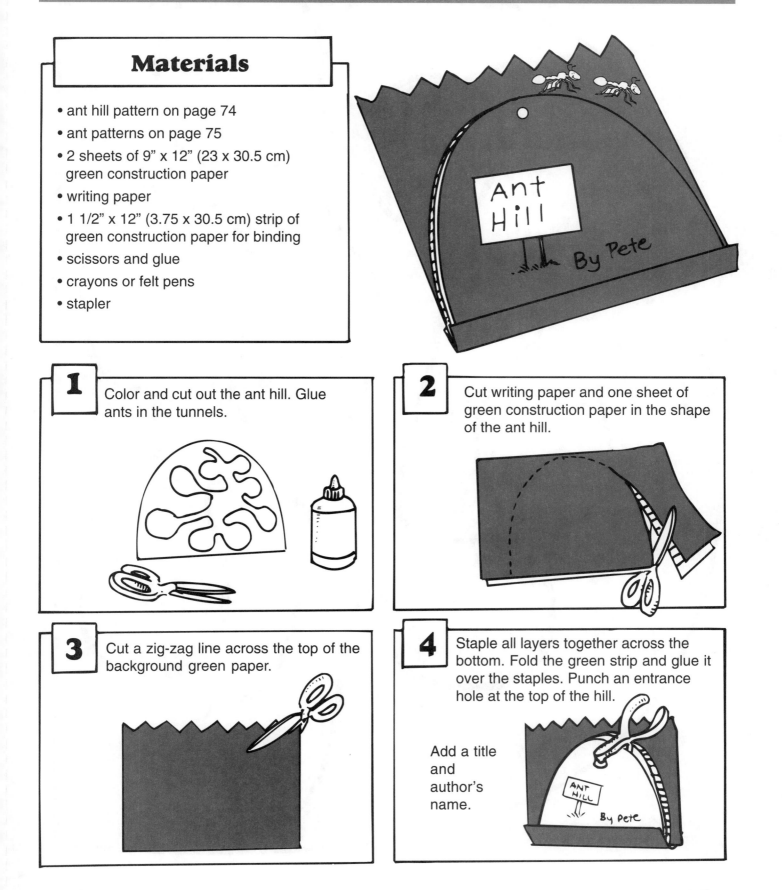

Materials

- ant hill pattern on page 74
- ant patterns on page 75
- 2 sheets of 9" x 12" (23 x 30.5 cm) green construction paper
- writing paper
- 1 1/2" x 12" (3.75 x 30.5 cm) strip of green construction paper for binding
- scissors and glue
- crayons or felt pens
- stapler

1 Color and cut out the ant hill. Glue ants in the tunnels.

2 Cut writing paper and one sheet of green construction paper in the shape of the ant hill.

3 Cut a zig-zag line across the top of the background green paper.

4 Staple all layers together across the bottom. Fold the green strip and glue it over the staples. Punch an entrance hole at the top of the hill.

Add a title and author's name.

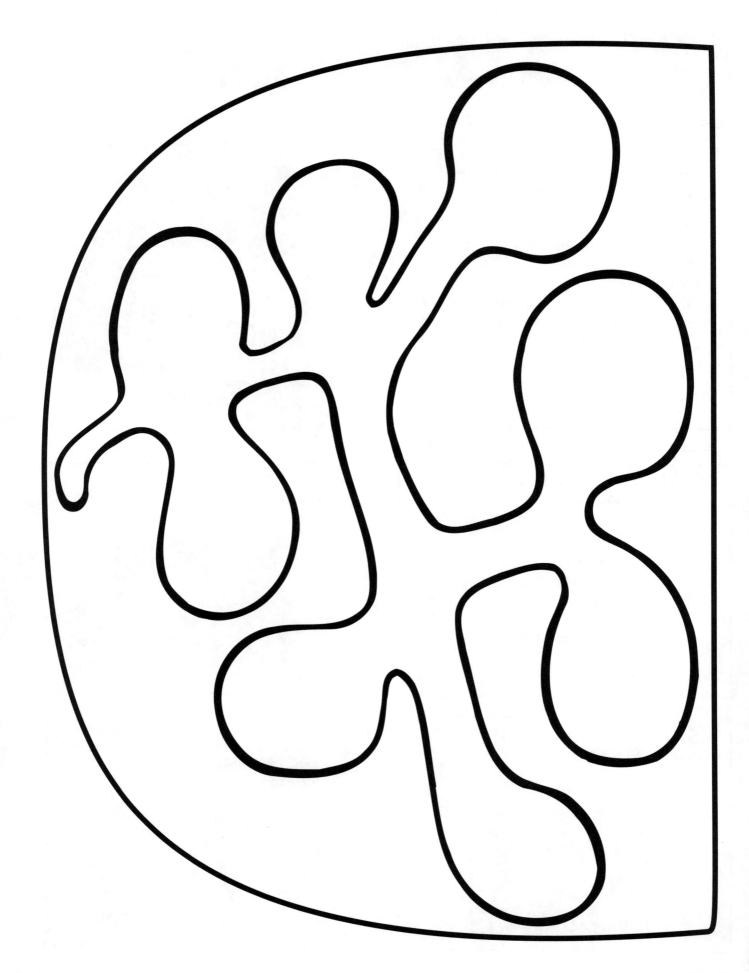

Read a Book, Make a Book EMC 778

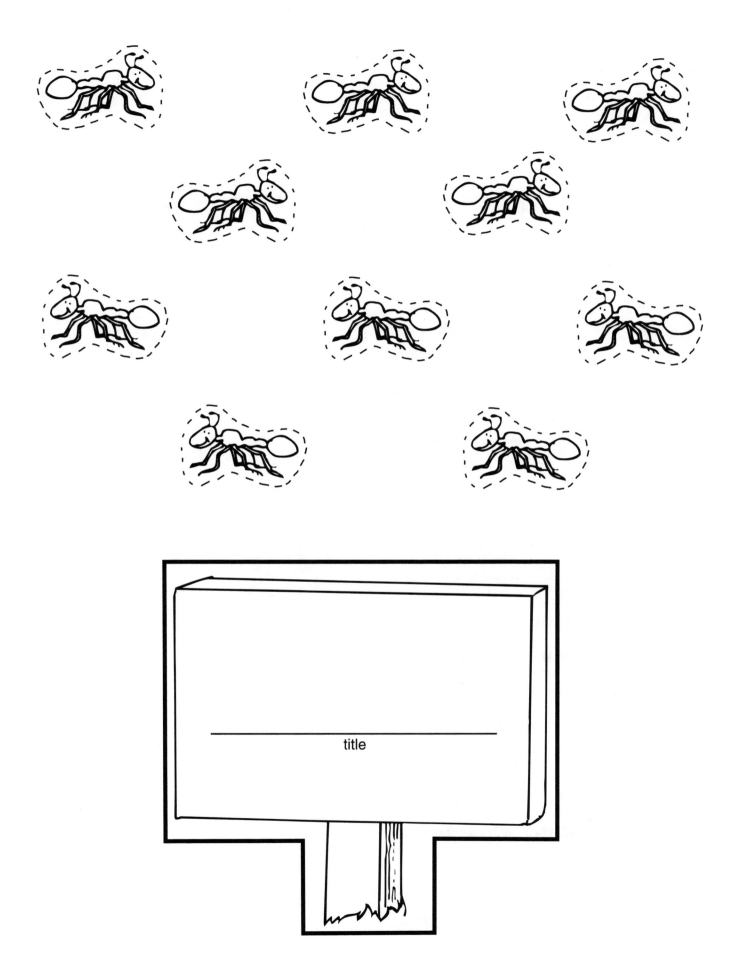

title

Read a Book, Make a Book EMC 778

Tops and Bottoms
by Janet Stevens; Harcourt Brace, 1995

Book Project

After You Read

1. Ask your students to name all the vegetables that they can. Write the ones that they name on a list.

2. Bring several examples of vegetables into the classroom—a head of lettuce, a carrot, a potato, some broccoli.

3. Determine whether you would rather have the top, middle, or bottom of the vegetables on your list. This many require some research. Encourage students to use seed catalogs, encyclopedias, and gardeners for assistance.

Now Write!

Retell the story of ***Tops and Bottoms*** using some of the vegetables on your list.

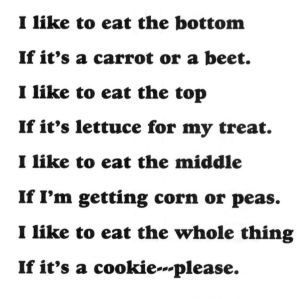

I like to eat the bottom

If it's a carrot or a beet.

I like to eat the top

If it's lettuce for my treat.

I like to eat the middle

If I'm getting corn or peas.

I like to eat the whole thing

If it's a cookie---please.

Jill Norris

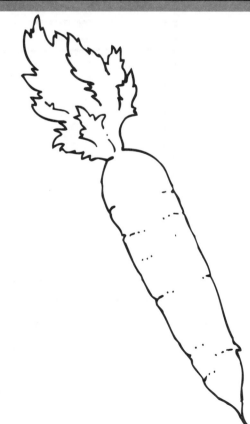

Read a Book, Make a Book EMC 778

Materials

• 12" x 18" (30.5 x 45.5 cm) brown construction paper

• tops and bottoms patterns on pages 78 and 79

• writing form on page 79

• scissors and glue

• crayons or felt pens

• 9" x 12" (23 x 30.5 cm) construction paper for covers

• hole punch

• metal rings

1 Fold brown construction paper. Trim 1" (2.5 cm) off the left margin. Glue the "Tops" and "Bottoms" signs to the construction paper flaps.

2 Color and cut out the plant parts. Glue the plant tops to the "tops" section so that they touch the edge of the flap.

Open the bottom section and glue the bottoms on the underneath section so they they line up with the tops.

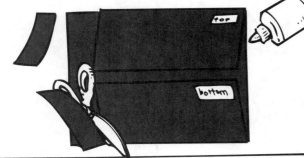

3 Glue the writing form under the top flap.

4 Collect student stories and add a cover. Punch holes in the left margin and insert metal rings.

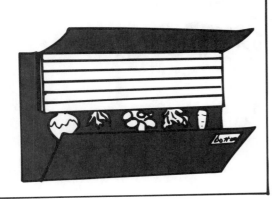

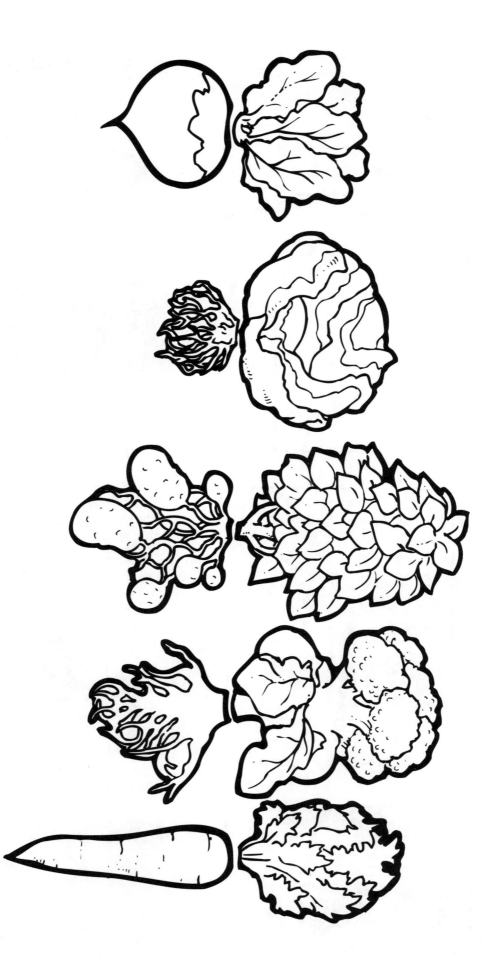

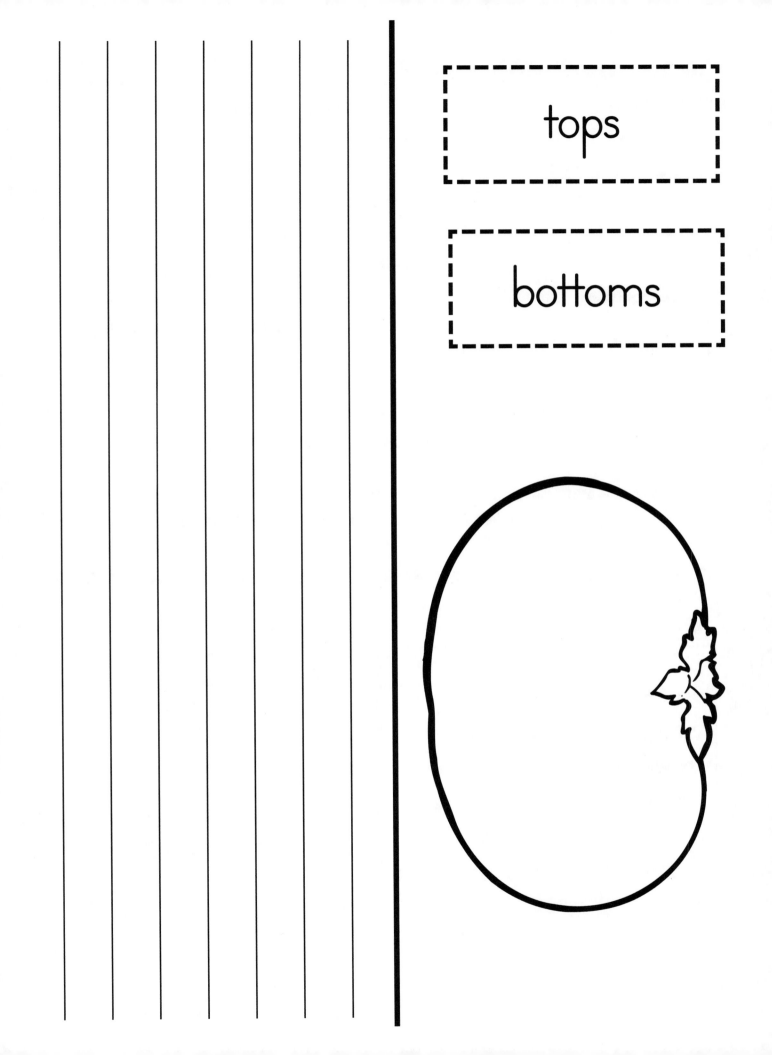

tops

bottoms

Orca Song

by Michael C. Armour; Smithsonian Oceanic Collection, 1994

Book Project

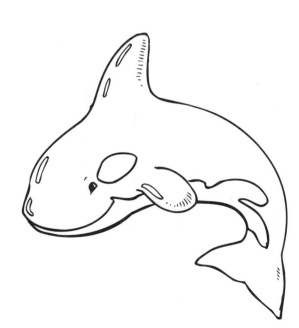

After You Read

1. Read more about orcas. The glossary and the notes at the end of *Orca Song* make a good starting point.

2. Discuss similes with your class. Point out the similes that Micheal Armour uses.

    "His lungs fill like balloons." (page 17)

    "Their songs of happiness race before them like ribbons of joy," (page 30)

Now Write!

Write similes about orcas that reflect the information you have learned.

The orca is like a thief when it steals salmon from the fishermen's nets.

The orca flips and turns,

The gymnast of the seas

It weighs four tons or more

But breaches with great ease.

Jill Norris

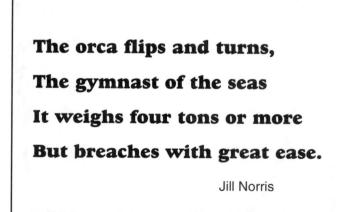

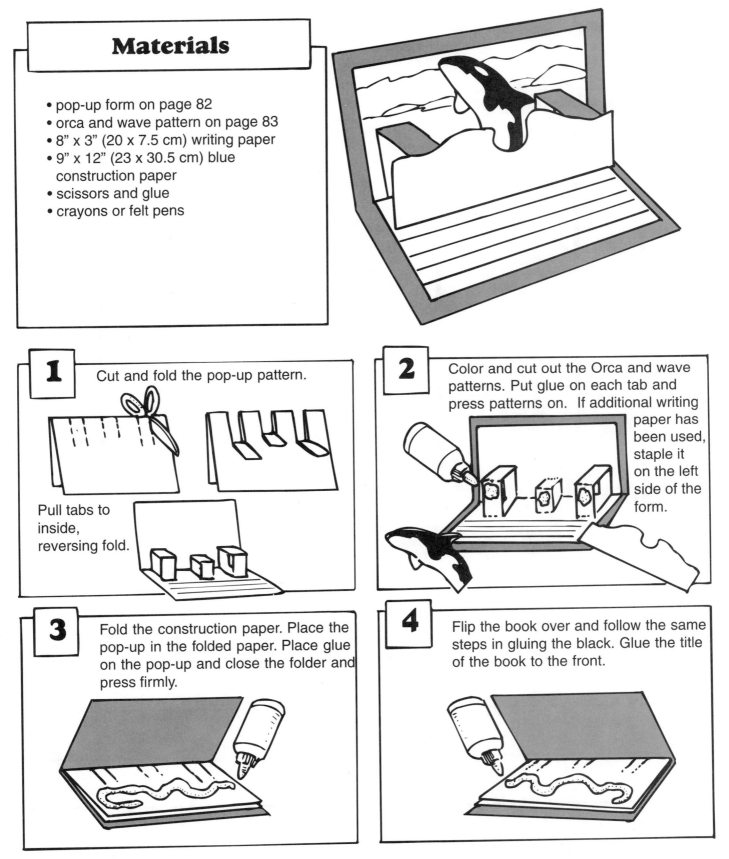

Materials

- pop-up form on page 82
- orca and wave pattern on page 83
- 8" x 3" (20 x 7.5 cm) writing paper
- 9" x 12" (23 x 30.5 cm) blue construction paper
- scissors and glue
- crayons or felt pens

1 Cut and fold the pop-up pattern.

Pull tabs to inside, reversing fold.

2 Color and cut out the Orca and wave patterns. Put glue on each tab and press patterns on. If additional writing paper has been used, staple it on the left side of the form.

3 Fold the construction paper. Place the pop-up in the folded paper. Place glue on the pop-up and close the folder and press firmly.

4 Flip the book over and follow the same steps in gluing the black. Glue the title of the book to the front.

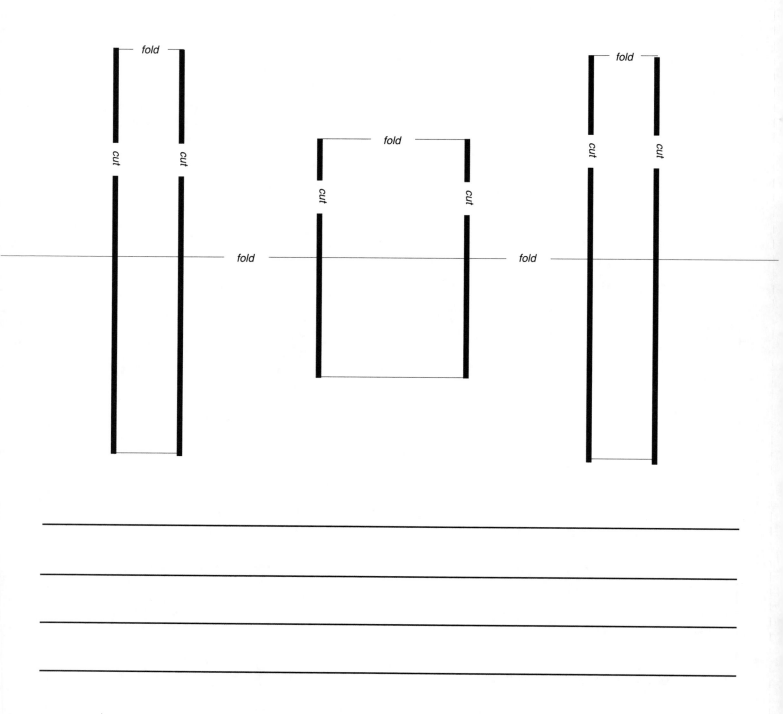

Orca

by:

Read a Book, Make a Book EMC 778

The Tale of Peter Rabbit

by Beatrix Potter; Dover Publications, 1972

Book Project

After You Read

Students may be interested in knowing that Beatrix Potter wrote stories about Peter Rabbit for a young friend who was sick. After reading the story discuss what students have learned about Peter's personality and character traits. What other kinds of things might a character like Peter do?

Now Write!

Write a new adventure for Peter. Be sure that he responds in appropriate ways.

Naughty little Peter

In MacGregor's peas,

You almost fooled the farmer

Until he heard you sneeze.

Hurry home to mother.

Next time use your head.

Don't go in the garden,

Go "berrying" instead.

Jill Norris

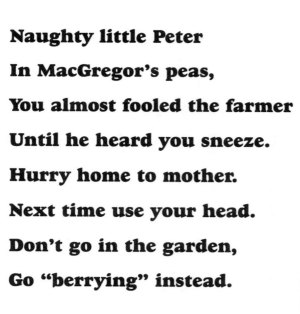

Rabbit in the Garden
Pop-Up Book

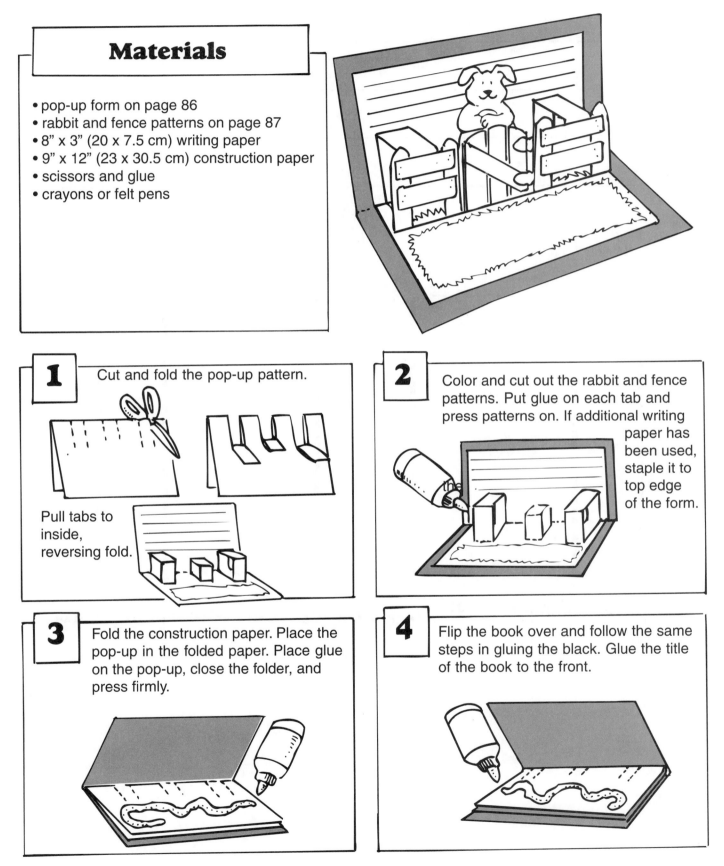

Materials

- pop-up form on page 86
- rabbit and fence patterns on page 87
- 8" x 3" (20 x 7.5 cm) writing paper
- 9" x 12" (23 x 30.5 cm) construction paper
- scissors and glue
- crayons or felt pens

1 Cut and fold the pop-up pattern.

Pull tabs to inside, reversing fold.

2 Color and cut out the rabbit and fence patterns. Put glue on each tab and press patterns on. If additional writing paper has been used, staple it to top edge of the form.

3 Fold the construction paper. Place the pop-up in the folded paper. Place glue on the pop-up, close the folder, and press firmly.

4 Flip the book over and follow the same steps in gluing the black. Glue the title of the book to the front.

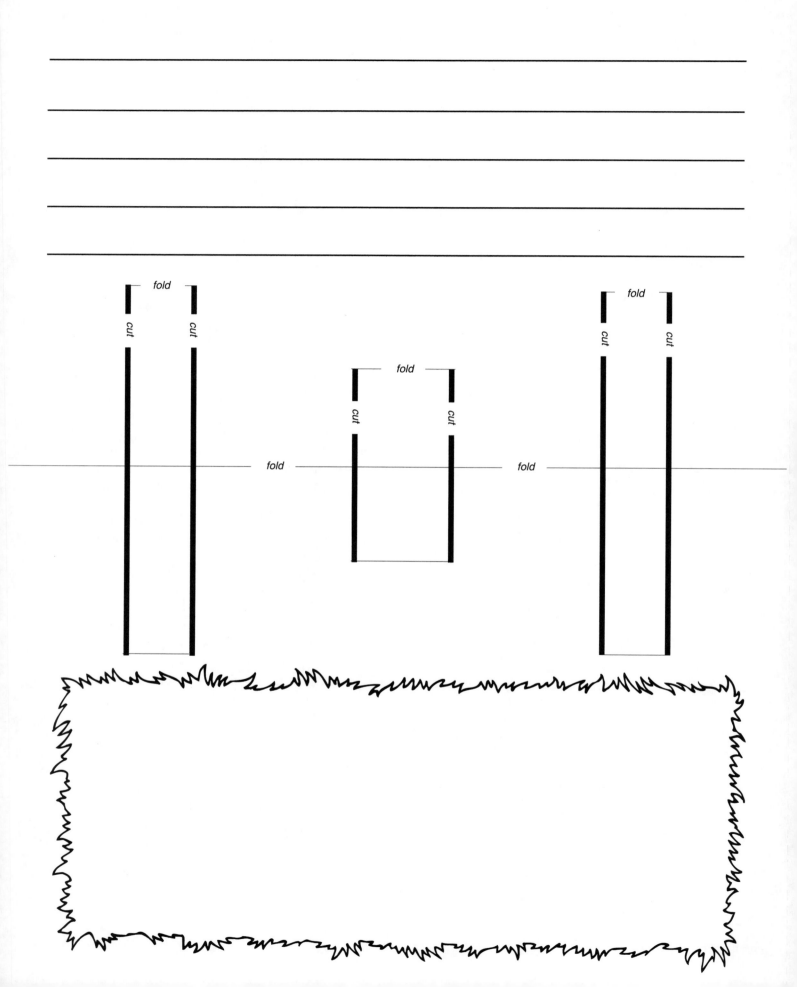

fold

cut

cut

fold

cut

cut

fold

fold

cut

cut

fold

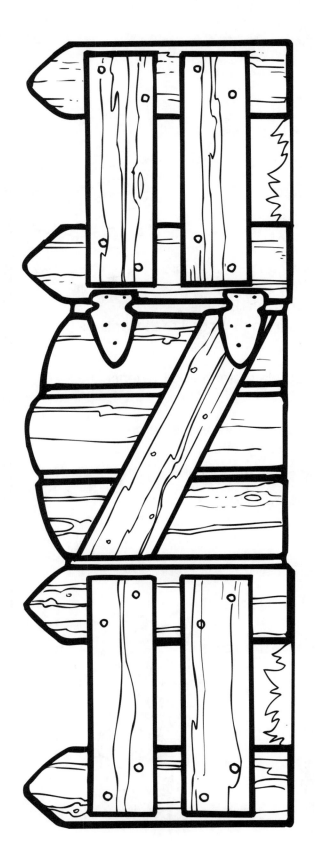

by:

Aesop's Fables

selected by Michael Hague; Holt, Rinehart, & Winston, 1985

Book Project

After You Read

This project is for older students. Younger groups can use the fable characters on page 91 to write about their favorite fable. Try a class fable before expecting students to write individual ones. For the best results, follow these steps to progress backwards from the moral to the writing.

1. Begin by choosing the moral.

   • Encourage students to select a lesson that relates to their experience.

   • State the moral clearly. For example:

   > Make sure that your tires are pumped up before you start on a trip.
   > Don't wear a white shirt when you eat spaghetti.

2. Select several animals to be the main characters in the story.

3. Think of a situation that would demonstrate the need for the lesson.

   A Vacation Bike Trek

   Giving a Speech after a Spaghetti Dinner

Now Write!

Write a new fable and create pop-up characters to illustrate it.

A fable is a story

With a moral at the end...

A lesson that the author

Would highly recommend.

Jill Norris

Make a Book...

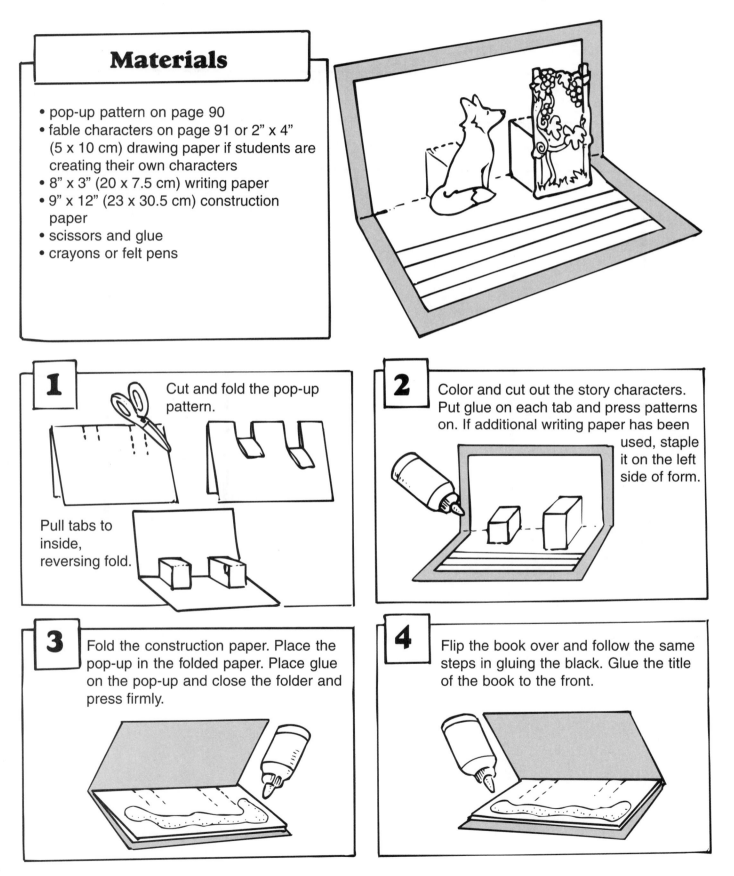

Materials

- pop-up pattern on page 90
- fable characters on page 91 or 2" x 4" (5 x 10 cm) drawing paper if students are creating their own characters
- 8" x 3" (20 x 7.5 cm) writing paper
- 9" x 12" (23 x 30.5 cm) construction paper
- scissors and glue
- crayons or felt pens

1 Cut and fold the pop-up pattern.

Pull tabs to inside, reversing fold.

2 Color and cut out the story characters. Put glue on each tab and press patterns on. If additional writing paper has been used, staple it on the left side of form.

3 Fold the construction paper. Place the pop-up in the folded paper. Place glue on the pop-up and close the folder and press firmly.

4 Flip the book over and follow the same steps in gluing the black. Glue the title of the book to the front.

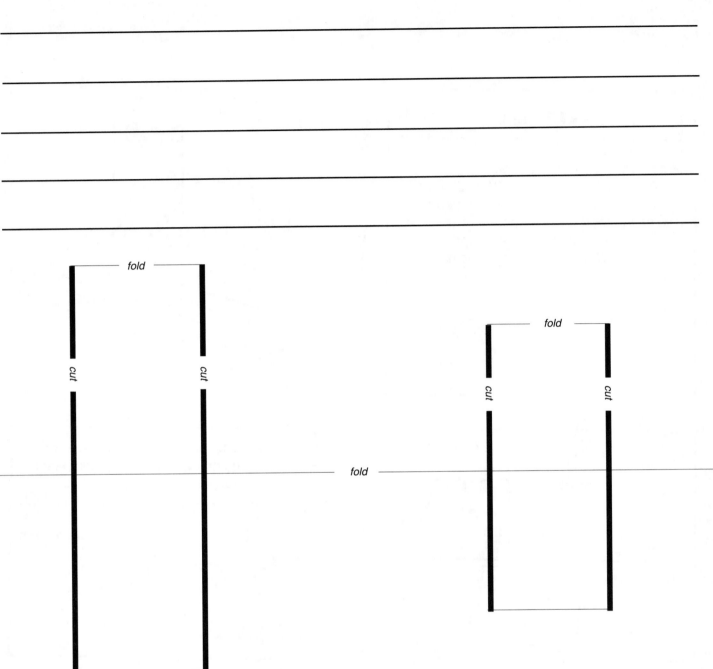

The Tortoise and
the Hare

by:

The Fox and
the Grapes

by:

Country Mouse
and City Mouse

by:

Thundercake

by Patricia Polocco; Philomel Books, 1990

Book Project

After You Read

The child and her grandmother make thundercake to keep them from thinking how scary the thunder and lightning are. Discuss with your students what they do when they are in a storm. After writing, extend the activity and let students talk about ways that they overcome other scary things.

Now Write!

Have students choose one idea and write about it. Encourage students to give their "Thundercake" a name.

> A Stormbuster
>
> Rain Song
>
> Hide and Seek Lightning

Clouds are boiling.

The sky is grey.

There's going to be

A storm today.

Grab your raincoat

And umbrella too.

Before you're soaked

All through and through.

Jill Norris

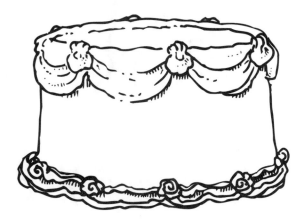

Make a Book...

Materials

- cloud patterns on page 94
- writing form on page 95
- 8" x 4 1/2" (20 x 11.5 cm) writing paper
- 9" x 12" (23 x 30.5 cm) blue construction paper
- scissors and glue
- crayons or felt pens

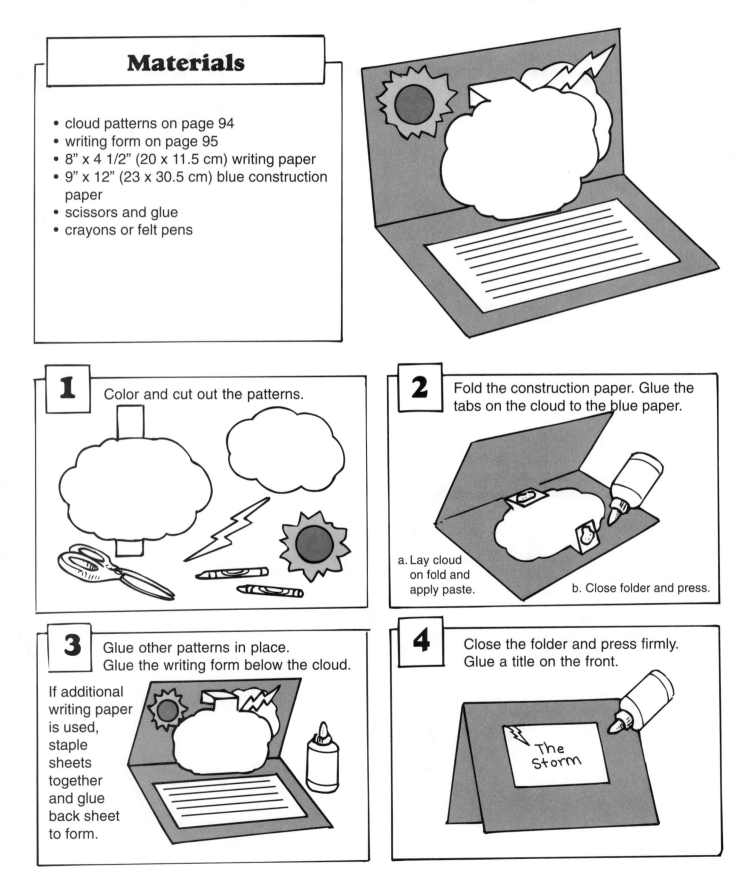

1 Color and cut out the patterns.

2 Fold the construction paper. Glue the tabs on the cloud to the blue paper.

a. Lay cloud on fold and apply paste.

b. Close folder and press.

3 Glue other patterns in place. Glue the writing form below the cloud.

If additional writing paper is used, staple sheets together and glue back sheet to form.

4 Close the folder and press firmly. Glue a title on the front.

The Storm

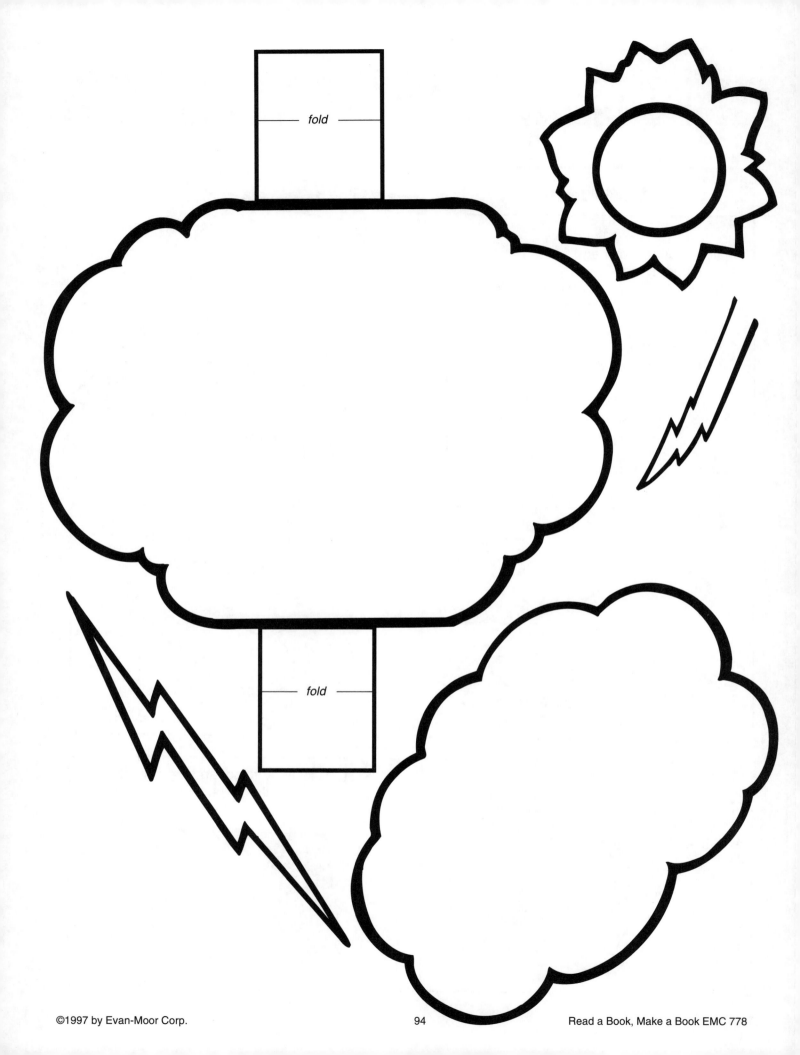

fold

fold

94

_____

title

_____

by

_____

_____

_____

_____

_____

_____

_____

Polar, the Titanic Bear

by Daisy Corning Stone Spedden; Little, Brown, 1994

Book Project

After You Read

The Titanic was the biggest ship in the world when it was built.

- It was 882 feet long—almost as long as four city blocks.
- It had nine decks and was as high as an eleven story building.
- Its three anchors weighed a total of 31 tons. (As much as 20 cars.)

Think about:

- How would it feel to be an oceanliner?
- What would you see?
- Where would you go?

Now Write!

Have students write a journal entry describing a day on their voyage.

A giant hotel upon the sea.
A special place for you and me.
Shining sun and ocean air
Watch the waves without a care.

Jill Norris

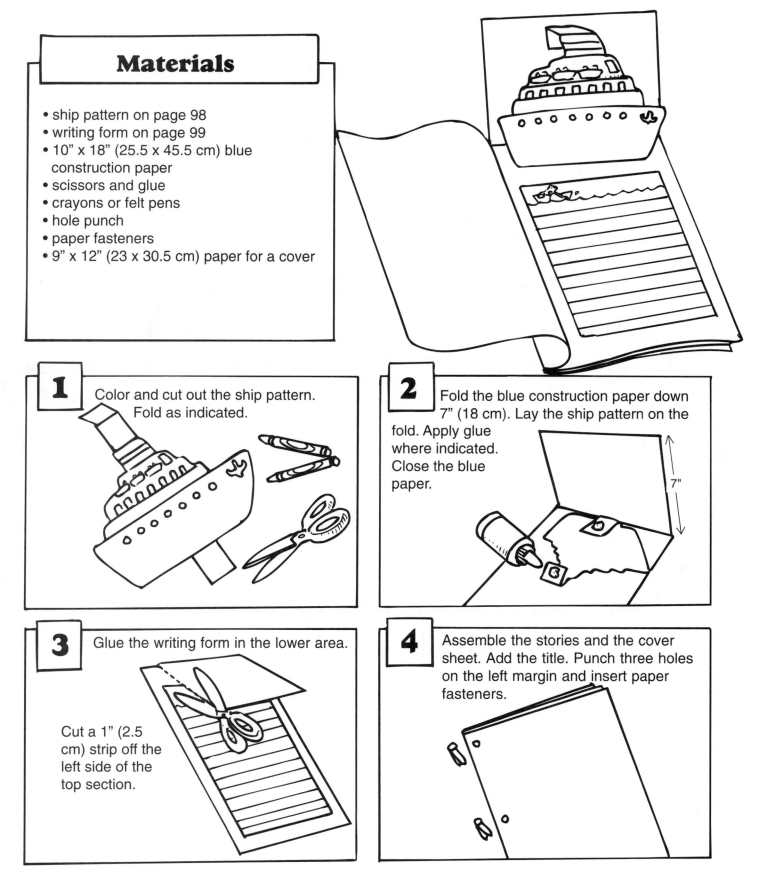

Materials

- ship pattern on page 98
- writing form on page 99
- 10" x 18" (25.5 x 45.5 cm) blue construction paper
- scissors and glue
- crayons or felt pens
- hole punch
- paper fasteners
- 9" x 12" (23 x 30.5 cm) paper for a cover

1 Color and cut out the ship pattern. Fold as indicated.

2 Fold the blue construction paper down 7" (18 cm). Lay the ship pattern on the fold. Apply glue where indicated. Close the blue paper.

7"

3 Glue the writing form in the lower area.

Cut a 1" (2.5 cm) strip off the left side of the top section.

4 Assemble the stories and the cover sheet. Add the title. Punch three holes on the left margin and insert paper fasteners.

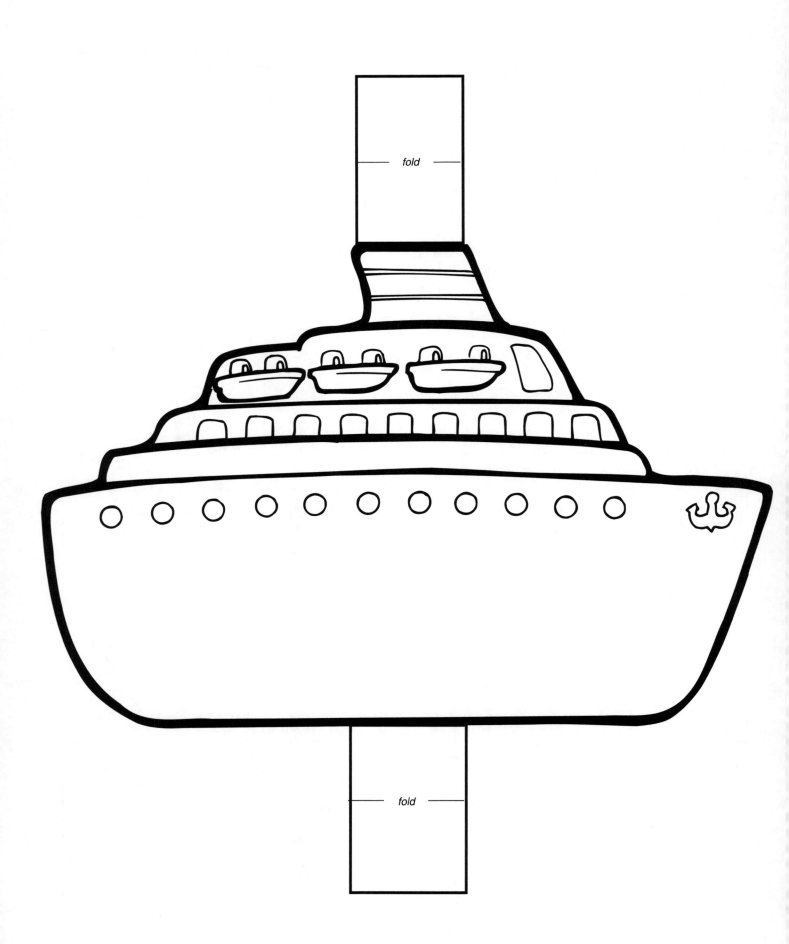

Read a Book, Make a Book EMC 778

_____

_____

_____

_____

_____

_____

_____

_____

_____

_____

_____

_____

_____

Truck

by Donald Crews; Greenwillow Books, 1980

Book Project

After You Read

1. Make a list of kinds of trucks and discuss their jobs.

2. Explain to students what a caption is:

    A caption describes what is happening in a photograph or a picture.

    A caption briefly gives important information.

3. Choose a truck. Use one of the patterns provided or draw one of your own. Mount it on the pop-up form as shown.

4. Find out what job your truck does and where it would work.

Now Write!

Write a caption telling about the truck's job.

Just like ants busy on their hill,

The trucks move in and about.

Loaded, then empty, they fill the holes

As cement pouts out of the spout.

Just like ants busy on their hill,

The trucks move in and about

Helping the people whose cars are stalled

Towing them up and out.

Jill Norris

Make a Book...

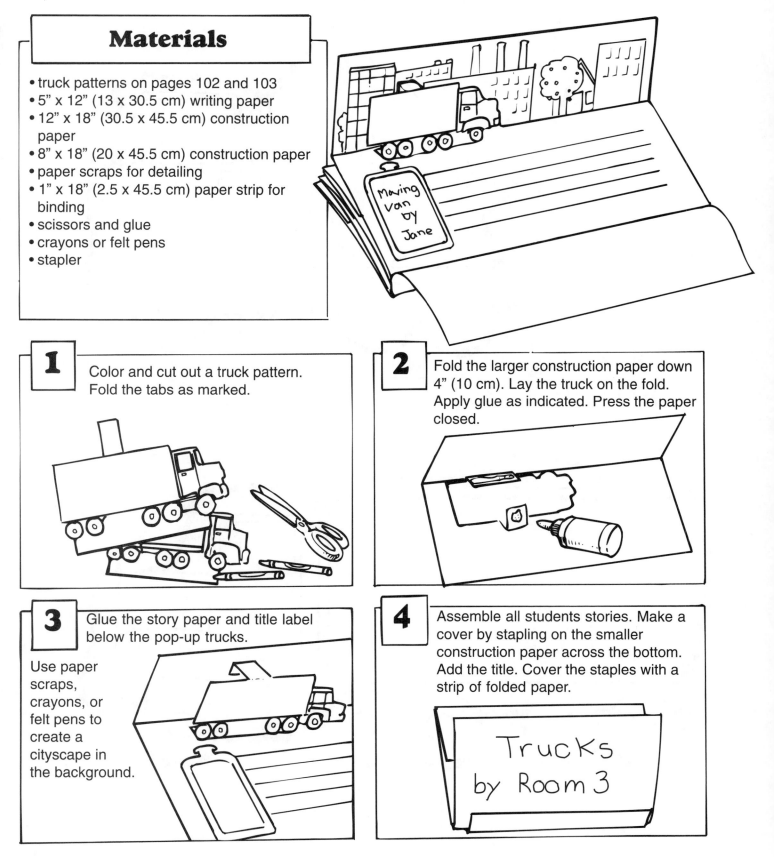

Materials

- truck patterns on pages 102 and 103
- 5" x 12" (13 x 30.5 cm) writing paper
- 12" x 18" (30.5 x 45.5 cm) construction paper
- 8" x 18" (20 x 45.5 cm) construction paper
- paper scraps for detailing
- 1" x 18" (2.5 x 45.5 cm) paper strip for binding
- scissors and glue
- crayons or felt pens
- stapler

1 Color and cut out a truck pattern. Fold the tabs as marked.

2 Fold the larger construction paper down 4" (10 cm). Lay the truck on the fold. Apply glue as indicated. Press the paper closed.

3 Glue the story paper and title label below the pop-up trucks.

Use paper scraps, crayons, or felt pens to create a cityscape in the background.

4 Assemble all students stories. Make a cover by stapling on the smaller construction paper across the bottom. Add the title. Cover the staples with a strip of folded paper.

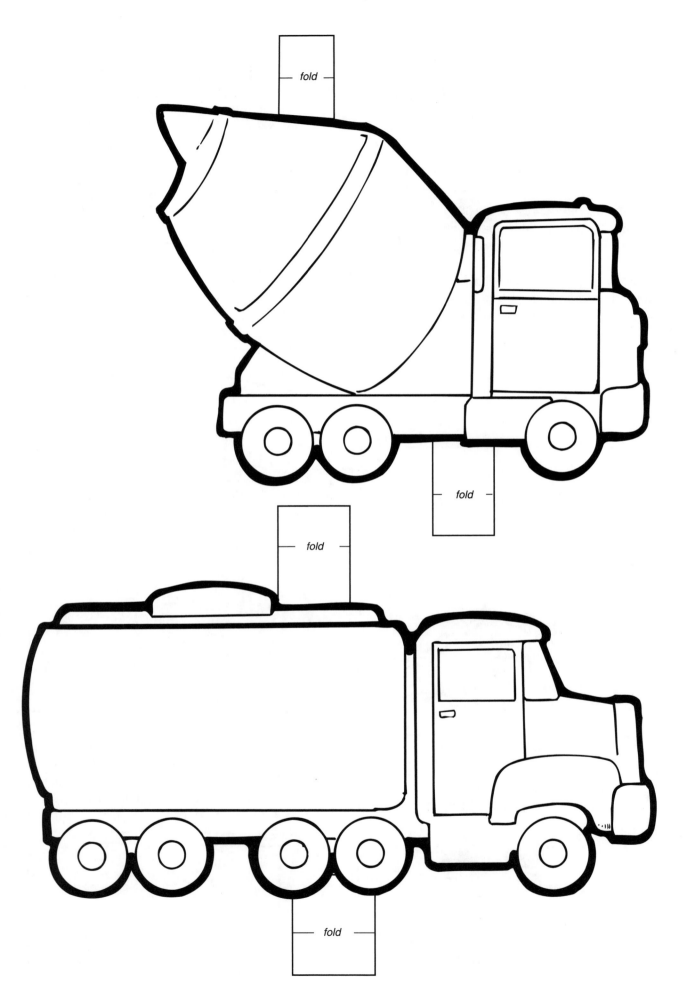

fold

fold

fold

fold

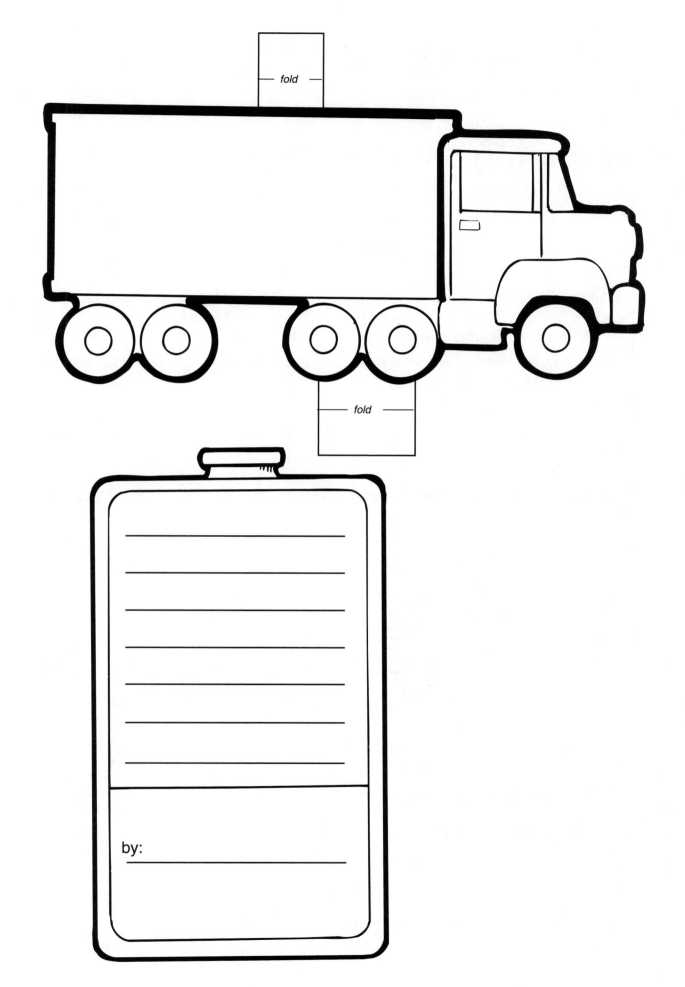

by: _____

103

Make Way for Ducklings
by Robert McCloskey; The Viking Press, 1941

Book Project

After You Read

1. Mr. and Mrs. Duck were looking for a place to nest. Discuss what they felt was important about a nesting area.

2. As a class, write an advertisement that describes a habitat that would be a good nesting place for a duck.

Now Write!

Have students write stories about the ducks who answer the advertisement and move in.

Watch the ducklings go

Waddling in a row.

Jill Norris

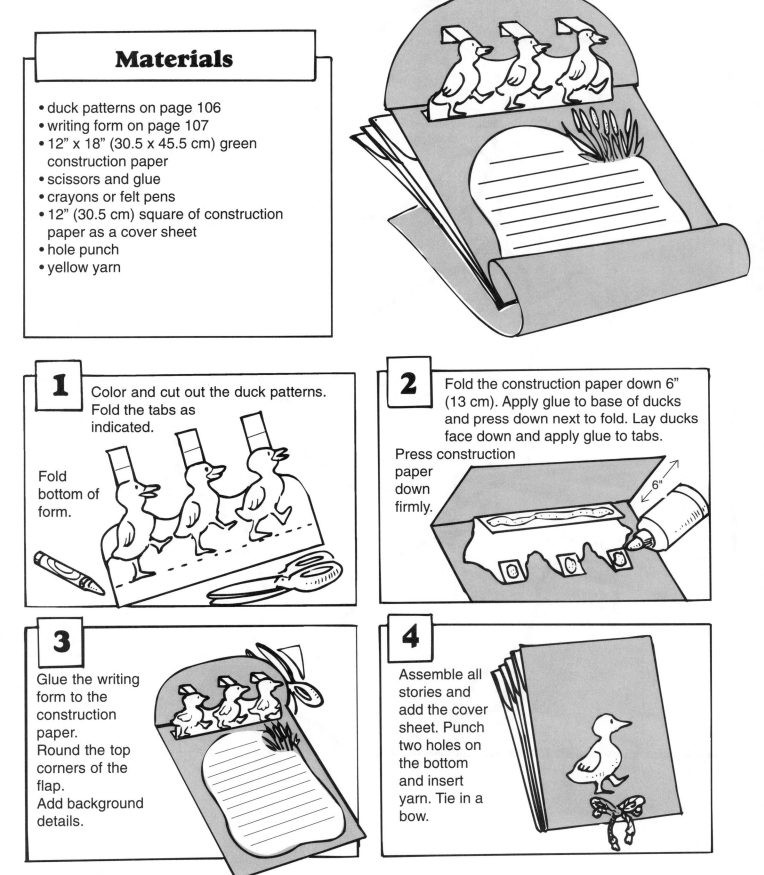

Materials

- duck patterns on page 106
- writing form on page 107
- 12" x 18" (30.5 x 45.5 cm) green construction paper
- scissors and glue
- crayons or felt pens
- 12" (30.5 cm) square of construction paper as a cover sheet
- hole punch
- yellow yarn

1 Color and cut out the duck patterns. Fold the tabs as indicated.

Fold bottom of form.

2 Fold the construction paper down 6" (13 cm). Apply glue to base of ducks and press down next to fold. Lay ducks face down and apply glue to tabs.

Press construction paper down firmly.

6"

3 Glue the writing form to the construction paper. Round the top corners of the flap. Add background details.

4 Assemble all stories and add the cover sheet. Punch two holes on the bottom and insert yarn. Tie in a bow.

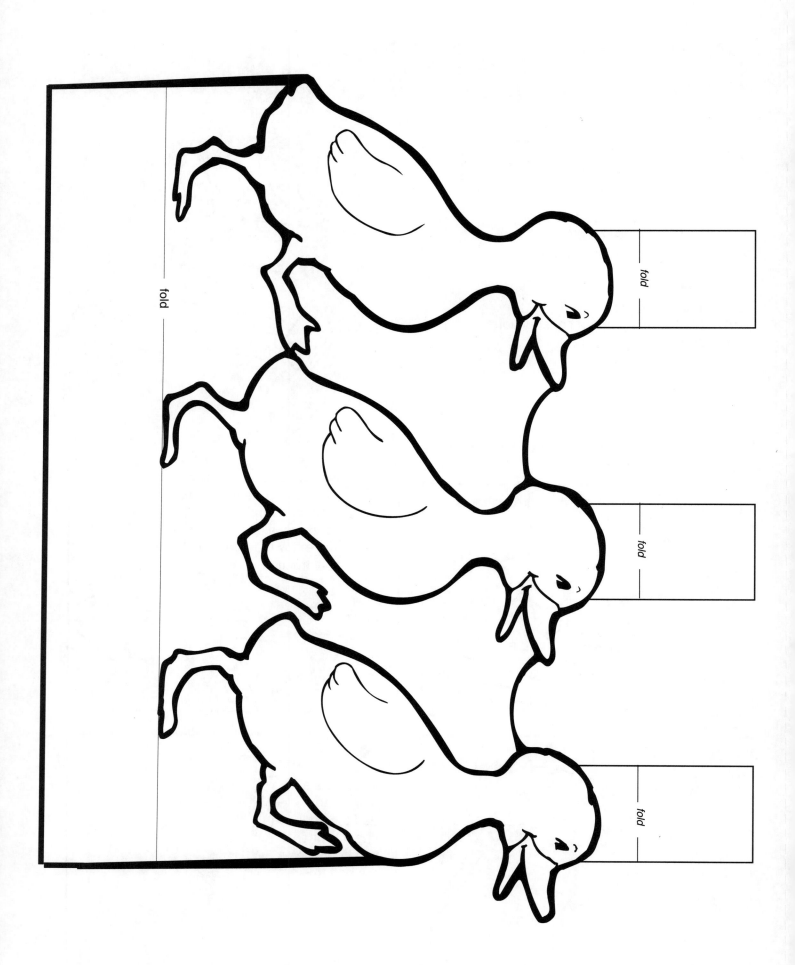

Read a Book, Make a Book EMC 778

_____

_____

_____

_____

_____

_____

_____

_____

_____

_____

Read a Book, Make a Book EMC 778

Garden for a Groundhog
by Lorna Ballian; Abingdon Press, 1985

Book Project

After You Read

Use a brown tube sock with button eyes to reenact the moment when the groundhog sticks its head above the ground after a winter of hibernation. Make sure each student has a chance to think of a response that the groundhog might make.

Now Write!

Imagine that groundhogs have kept a record of all the Groundhog Days through the years. Write an entry for this record describing this year's Groundhog Day.

I'm afraid to look out

After winter inside.

It's easier by far

To stay here and hide.

But spring's warmth calls,

I must take a peek.

Let's see now...what's up here?

Oh, a shadow...EEEEKKKKKK!

Jill Norris

Materials

- 10" x 18" (25.5 x 45.5 cm) blue construction paper
- groundhog pop-up on page 110
- writing form and patterns on page 111
- scissors and glue
- crayons or felt pens
- 10" x 12" (25.5 x 30.5 cm) piece of construction paper for cover
- hole punch
- twine

1 Color, cut, and fold the pop-up pattern.

2 Fold the blue paper over 6" (15cm). Lay the pop-up on the fold and apply glue. Close the folder and press. Flip the book over and repeat gluing on other side.

6" (15 cm)

3 Glue the writing form next to the groundhog.

4 Assemble all pages and add a cover. Punch two holes on the left side and tie with twine.

Groundhog Journal

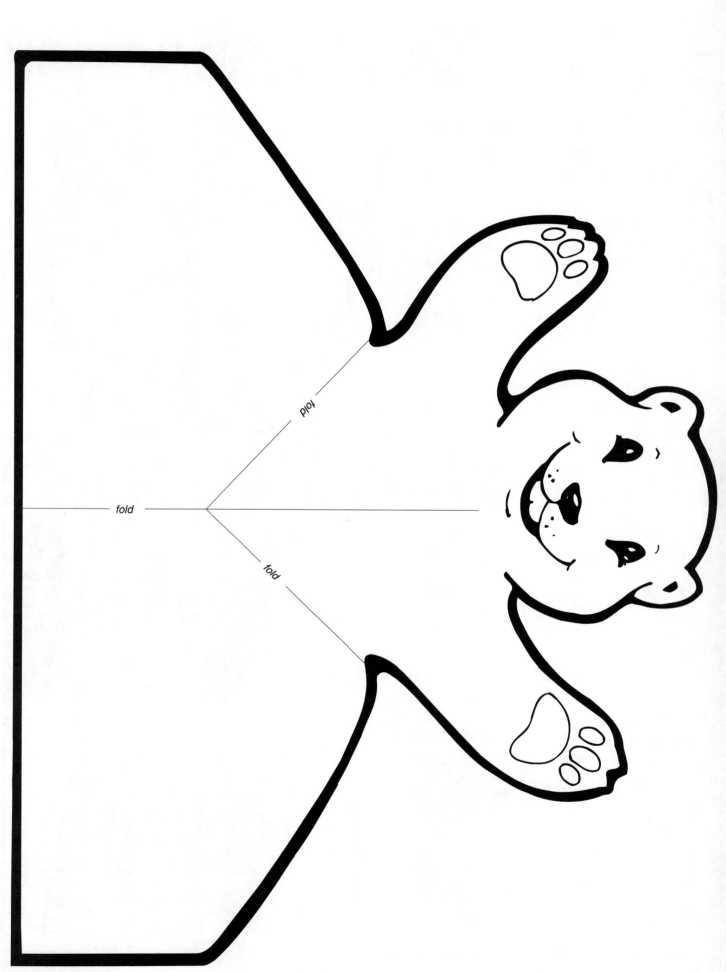

fold

fold

fold

Groundhog Day

_____
date

Weather

Sunny   Cloudy   Partly Sunny

Rainy   Stormy

Observers

_____

_____

An Account of What Happened

_____

_____

_____

_____

_____

_____
signed

 Read a Book, Make a Book EMC 778

A Flea in the Ear
by Stephen Wyllie; Dutton Children's Books, 1995

Book Project

After You Read

When students write for this book project they will be assuming the roles of reporters. Discuss the "5 Ws" of reporting: Who, What, Where, When, Why (and How).

Relate the "5 Ws" to the story of Spotted Hound.

Now Write!

- Have students pretend to be a reporter and record the events of this story in a newspaper account.
- Tell all the facts.

Bouncing, pouncing pup

Running, sunning pup

Licking, tricking pup

Wiggling, jiggling pup

Napping, scrapping pup

You are my pick-me-up!

Jill Norris

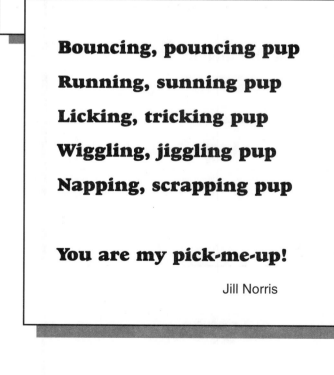

112   Read a Book, Make a Book EMC 778

Make a Book...

Dog
Pop-Up Book

Materials

- dog pattern on page 114
- writing form on page 115
- 12" x 15" (30.5 x 38 cm) construction paper
- scissors and glue
- crayons or felt pens
- stapler
- 12" (30.5 cm) square of construction paper for a cover sheet
- 1" x 12" (2.5 x 30.5 cm) strip of construction paper for binding

1 Color and cut out the dog pattern. Follow folding directions.

2 Fold the construction paper up 3" (7.5 cm) on the end. Put glue on the dog's paws. Position the dog's feet on either side of the fold 1" (2.5 cm) away. Close the folded paper. Press firmly.

3 Glue the writing form to the construction paper. Leave room for a binding across the top edge.

4 Collect student stories and add a decorated cover sheet. Staple across the top and cover with a strip of folded paper.

Read a Book, Make a Book EMC 778

fold

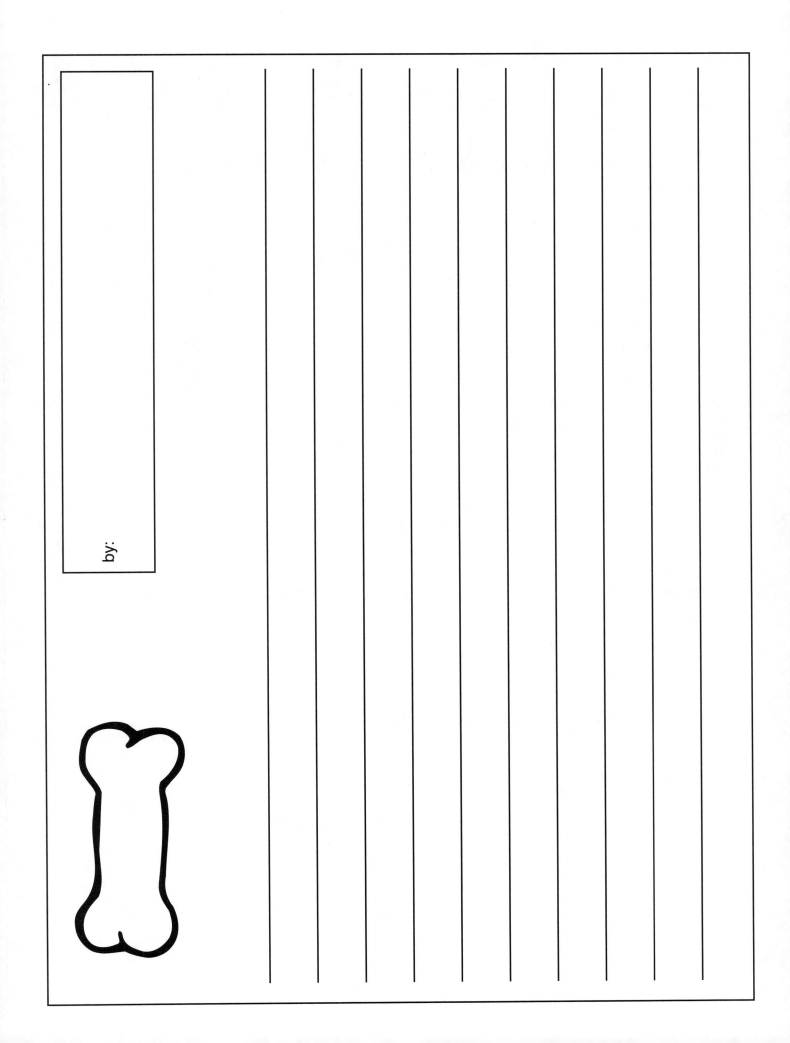

by:

Three Days on a River in a Red Canoe

by Vera B. Williams; Greenwillow Books, 1981

Book Project

After You Read

1. Set up a camp at school.

   - Pitch a tent

   - Cook a snack on a cookstove

   - Turn off the lights and use flashlights for reading in the tent

   - Tell stories around a "campfire"

   - Listen to recordings of wild animal sounds

Now Write!

Write a comparison about a day camping out and a day at home. Tell the things that are similar and the things that are different.

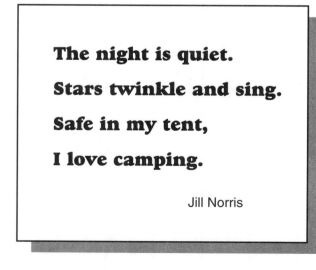

> The night is quiet.
>
> Stars twinkle and sing.
>
> Safe in my tent,
>
> I love camping.
>
> Jill Norris

Read a Book, Make a Book EMC 778

Make a Book...

Materials

- tent pattern on page 118
- 5" x 7" (13 x 18 cm) piece of brown construction paper for the tent flap
- writing form on page 119
- scissors and glue
- crayons and felt pens
- 12" x 18" (30.5 x 45.5 cm) blue construction paper
- stapler
- 1" x 12" (2.5 x 30 5 cm) constuction paper strip for binding

1

Color and cut out the tent. Glue the top edge of the brown paper in place as the tent flap.

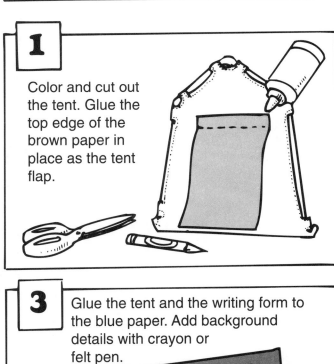

2

Lift the flap and draw what is inside the tent.

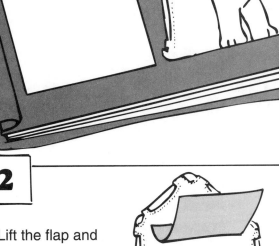

3

Glue the tent and the writing form to the blue paper. Add background details with crayon or felt pen.

4

Collect student stories and add a cover sheet. Decorate to support the story theme. Staple on the left and cover with a folded paper strip.

Read a Book, Make a Book EMC 778

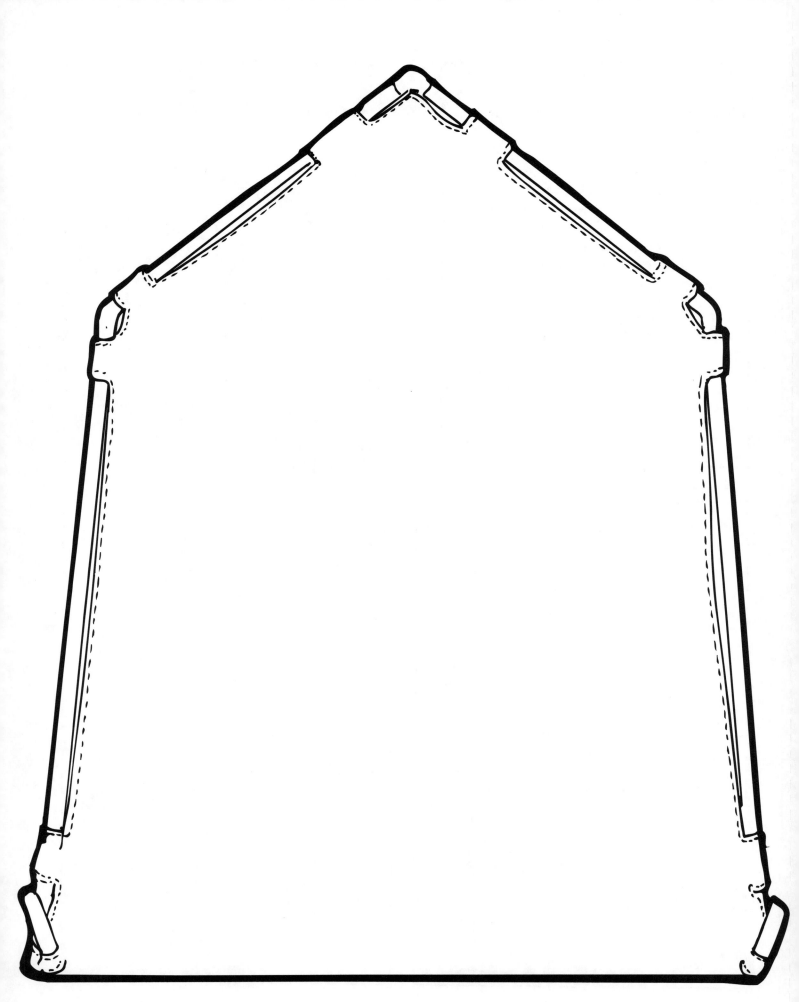

Read a Book, Make a Book EMC 778

The Doorbell Rang

by Pat Hutchins; Greenwillow Books, 1986

Book Project

After You Read

1. Discuss things that students do inside their houses.

   • eating breakfast

   • practicing piano

   • taking a bath

2. Choose one event and imagine that the doorbell rings while this is going on. Who will be at the door? What will that person say?

Now Write!

Give the "ringer" a speech bubble and a response. Write a description of what is going on.

> Good morning!

> Is that dinner I smell?

> I thought I heard a call for help.

Just when I'm sure
No one will stir.
The doorbell rings.

The baby's asleep.
Now I can sweep.
The doorbell rings.

The floor is drying.
I'm beddy-bying.
The doorbell rings.

Jill Norris

Read a Book, Make a Book EMC 778

Make a Book...

Materials

- door pattern on page 122
- construction paper door flap cut to 4" x 5 3/4" (10 x 14.5 cm)
- writing form on page 123
- 12" x 18" (30.5 x 45.5 cm) construction paper
- scissors and glue
- crayons or felt pens
- hole punch
- ribbon

1 Glue the left edge of the door flap to the pattern page.

Draw and color the details.

2 Glue the pattern to the construction paper. Open the door flap and draw who is at the door.

3 Cut out the writing form and paste it to the construction paper.

4 Put student pages together and add a cover sheet. Punch holes along the left and secure with ribbon.

Who's There?

Read a Book, Make a Book EMC 778

Goggles

by Ezra Jack Keats; Macmillan, 1969

Book Project

After You Read

Peter watched Willie and then the big boys through the fence. Let students talk about what's behind their fences. Make a list and add descriptive words.

Now Write!

Write a riddle as a clue. See if someone can read the riddle and guess what's behind the fence.

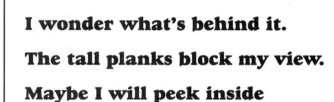

I wonder what's behind it.

The tall planks block my view.

Maybe I will peek inside

That's an easy thing to do.

Jill Norris

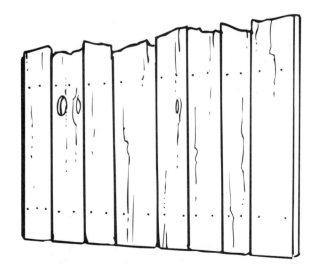

Read a Book, Make a Book EMC 778

Make a Book...

Materials

- fence pattern on page 126
- writing form on page 127
- answer folder on page 127
- 9" x 12" (30.5 x 45.5 cm) construction paper
- scissors and glue
- crayons and felt pens
- stapler
- 1" x 9" (2.5 x 23 cm) paper strip for binding

1 Color and cut out the fence pattern. Fold as indicated. Fold the fence down and draw the surprise behind.

2 Fold the fence back up and decide where to cut a "peek" hole. Paste the fence to the construction paper.

3 Cut out the riddle form and the answer folder. Paste them to the construction paper.

4 Collect student papers and add a cover sheet. Staple on the left margin and cover staples with a folded paper strip.

Behind My Fence by Room 23

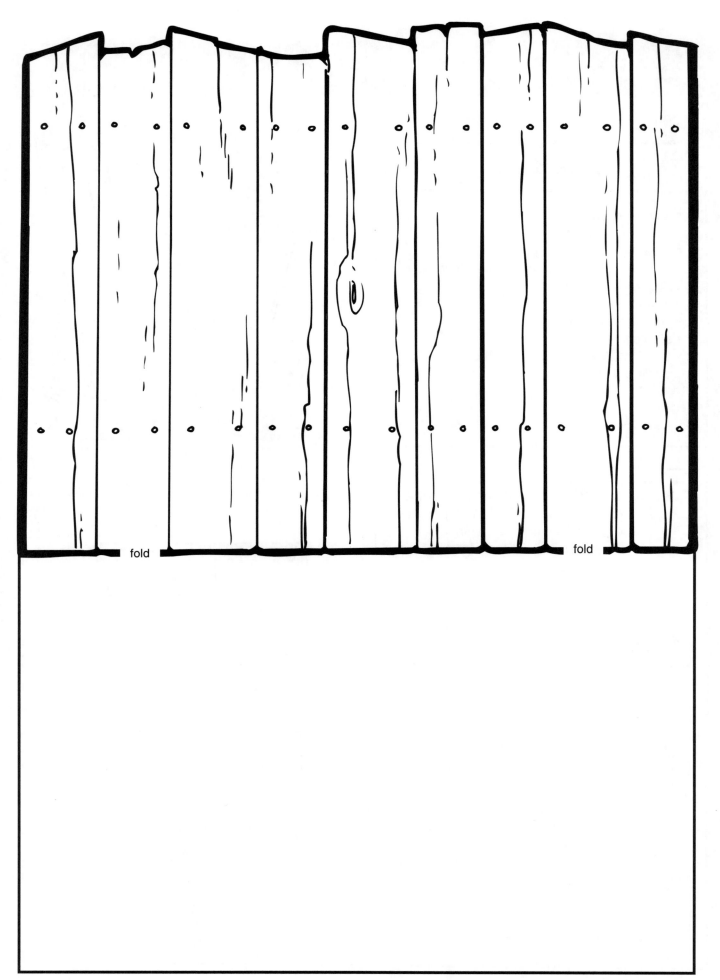

fold   fold

 Read a Book, Make a Book EMC 778

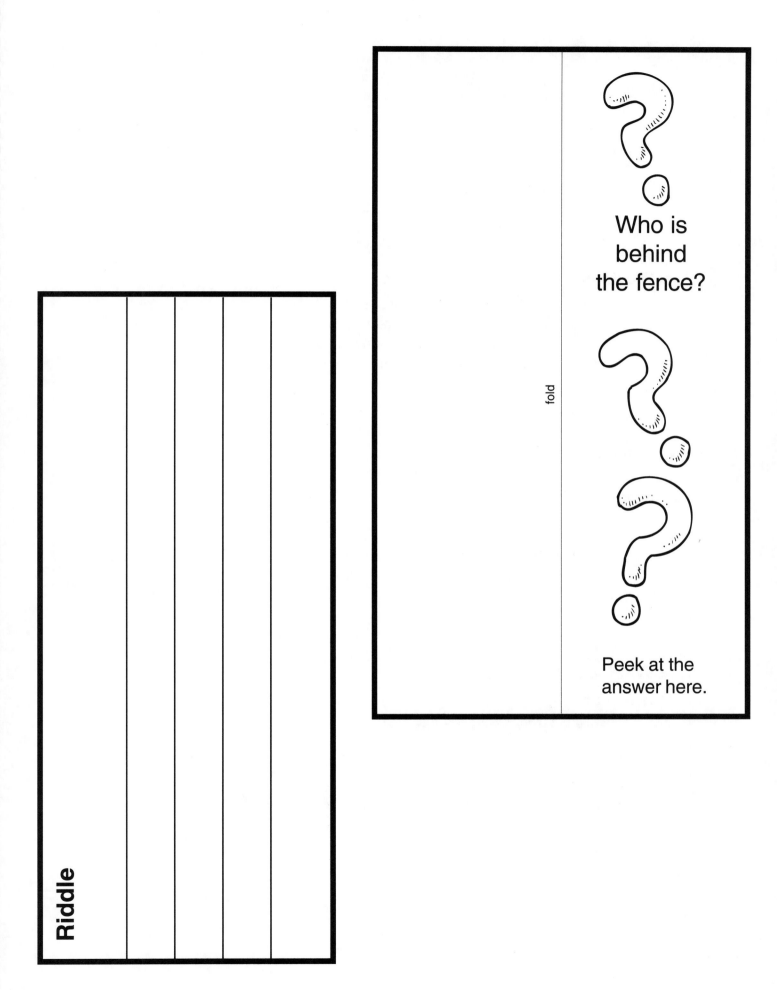

Riddle

Who is
behind
the fence?

fold

Peek at the
answer here.

Read a Book, Make a Book EMC 778

Frederick

by Leo Lionni; Pantheon, 1967

Book Project

After You Read

Frederick was a poet and used words to help his family live through the winter. Be like Frederick and gather words and images to record an event or a special occasion. Guide students in a discussion of pleasant memories. Make a list and add descriptive words and phrases. For example:

Family picnic
giggles and laughs, watermelon juice on my chin, a splash in a cool pool

Baby brother
soft skin, quiet gurgles, new baby scent

Now Write!

Record your images and feelings and store them away for gray days.

Gather colors.

Gather sounds.

   Store them safe for gray days.

Gather smells.

Gather tastes.

   They will be your bouquets.

Gather smiles.

Gather hugs.

   They will warm the cold days.

Gather memories.

Gather friends.

   They'll be with you always.

Jill Norris

Make a Book...

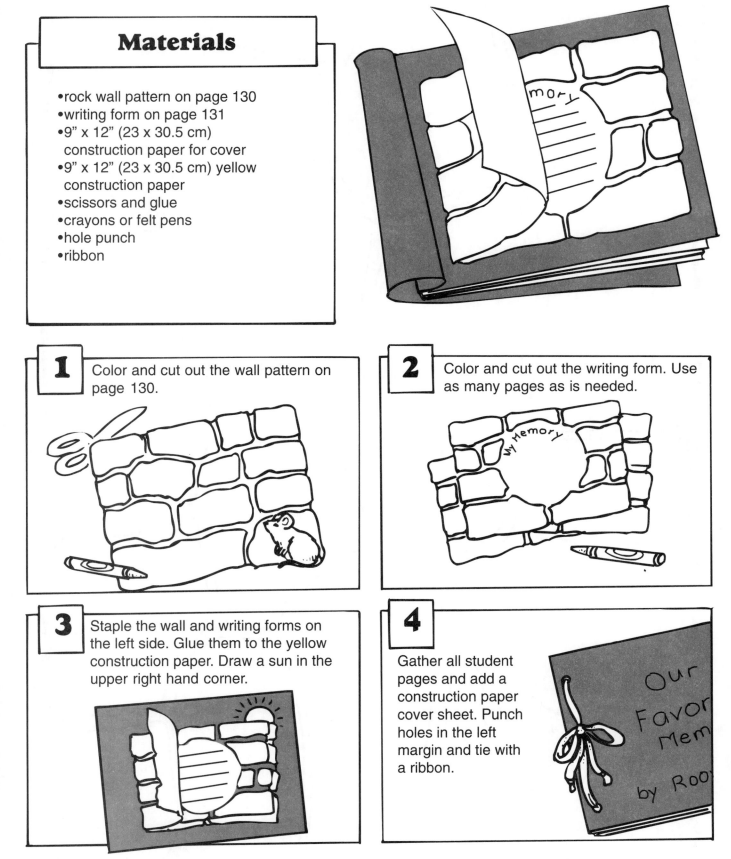

Materials

- rock wall pattern on page 130
- writing form on page 131
- 9" x 12" (23 x 30.5 cm) construction paper for cover
- 9" x 12" (23 x 30.5 cm) yellow construction paper
- scissors and glue
- crayons or felt pens
- hole punch
- ribbon

1 Color and cut out the wall pattern on page 130.

2 Color and cut out the writing form. Use as many pages as is needed.

3 Staple the wall and writing forms on the left side. Glue them to the yellow construction paper. Draw a sun in the upper right hand corner.

4 Gather all student pages and add a construction paper cover sheet. Punch holes in the left margin and tie with a ribbon.

Name: _____

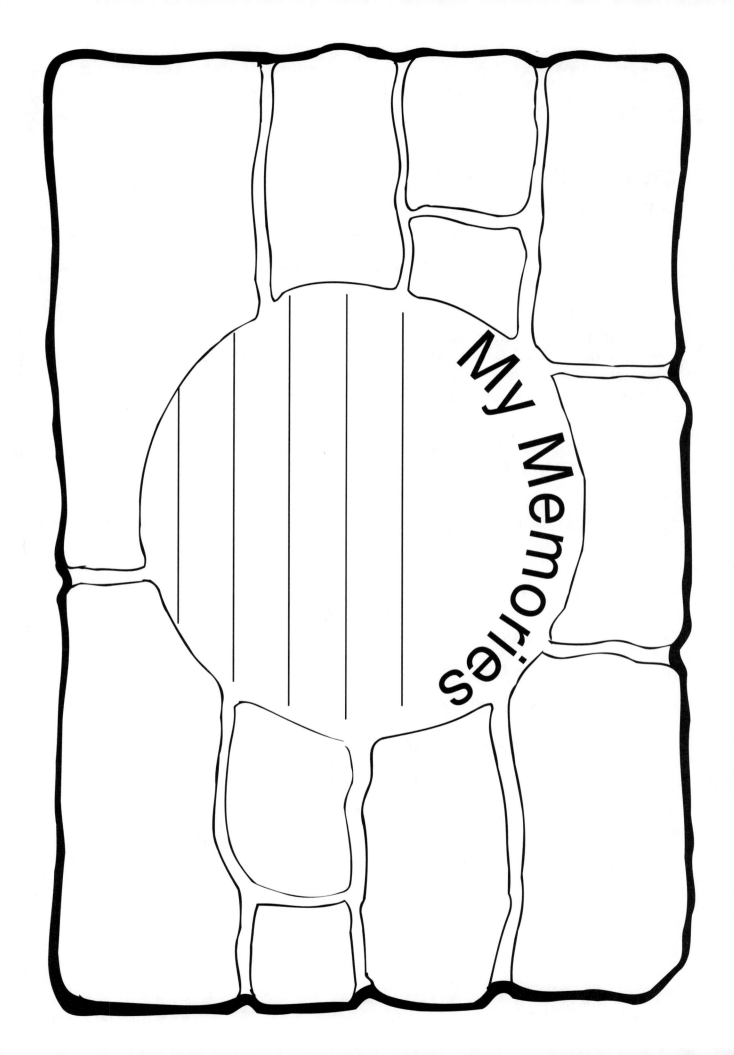

My Memories

Seven Blind Mice

by Ed Young; Philomel Books, 1991

Book Project

After You Read

Talk about how it's easy to get the wrong idea about something if your information is limited. Depending on the level of your students, extend this concept to judging people or situations. Let students share experiences where something was not what it seemed.

Now Write!

Students decide on a mystery object they wish to hide. These can be drawn or cut from magazines. Write riddles that reveal clues to the object's identity.

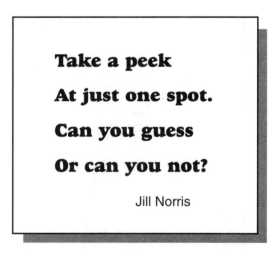

Take a peek

At just one spot.

Can you guess

Or can you not?

Jill Norris

Materials

- frame pattern on page 134
- writing form on page 135
- 6" x 9" (15 x 23 cm) white construction paper
- 12" x 18" (30.5 x 45.5 cm) colored construction paper
- scissors and glue
- crayons or felt pens
- stapler
- 1" x 12" (2.5 x 30.5 cm) strip of paper for binding cut with pinking shears

1 Draw and color the mystery picture in the frame or glue the photo in place.

2 Glue the mystery picture and the writing form on the large construction paper.

3 Paste the left edge of the white construction paper over the image in the mystery frame. Cut a quarter size circle as a peek hole.

4 Assemble student riddles and add a cover sheet decorated with question marks. Staple the book on the left margin and glue the folded paper over the staples.

Can You Guess?

_____

_____

_____

_____

_____

_____

_____

_____

_____

Name: _____

Read a Book, Make a Book EMC 778

Bread and Jam for Frances

by Russell Hoban; Harper & Row, 1964

Book Project

After You Read

Brainstorm and list students' favorite foods. Compile a word bank of descriptive words and phrases categorized by "How It Looks," "How It Tastes," "How It Smells."

Now Write!

Students write a description of their favorite food or food combination using words that create mental pictures.

What's that on your plate?

Is it steak or grilled fish?

Roast turkey with dressing?

What a beautiful dish!

Could it be green beans?

Cauliflower with cheese?

Peach pie a la mode?

Won't you give me some, please?

Jill Norris

Make a Book...

Materials

- writing form on page 138
- cover sheet on page 139
- 10" (25.5 cm) paper plate
- yarn or string
- a plastic spoon
- scissors
- crayons or felt pen
- stapler
- hole punch

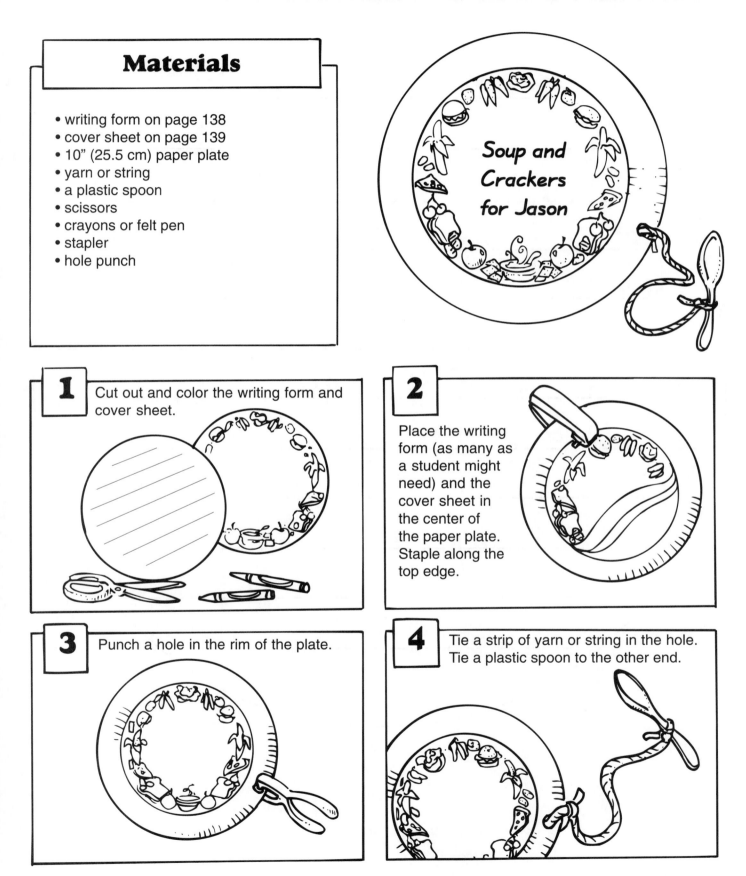

Soup and Crackers for Jason

1 Cut out and color the writing form and cover sheet.

2 Place the writing form (as many as a student might need) and the cover sheet in the center of the paper plate. Staple along the top edge.

3 Punch a hole in the rim of the plate.

4 Tie a strip of yarn or string in the hole. Tie a plastic spoon to the other end.

       Read a Book, Make a Book EMC 778

Read a Book, Make a Book EMC 778

for

The 500 Hats of Bartholomew Cubbins

by Dr. Seuss; Collins, 1966

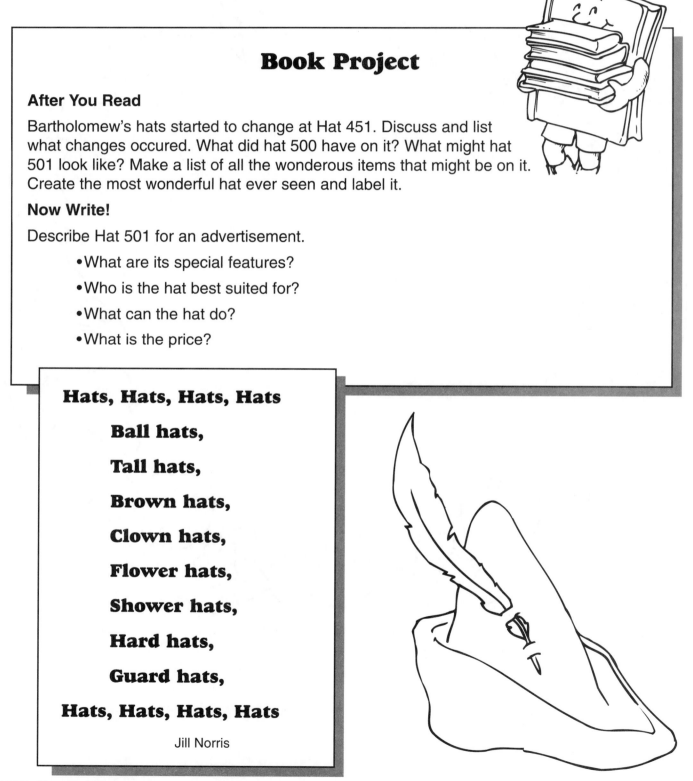

Book Project

After You Read

Bartholomew's hats started to change at Hat 451. Discuss and list what changes occured. What did hat 500 have on it? What might hat 501 look like? Make a list of all the wonderous items that might be on it. Create the most wonderful hat ever seen and label it.

Now Write!

Describe Hat 501 for an advertisement.

- •What are its special features?
- •Who is the hat best suited for?
- •What can the hat do?
- •What is the price?

Hats, Hats, Hats, Hats

Ball hats,

Tall hats,

Brown hats,

Clown hats,

Flower hats,

Shower hats,

Hard hats,

Guard hats,

Hats, Hats, Hats, Hats

Jill Norris

Read a Book, Make a Book EMC 778

Materials

- hat pattern on page 142
- hat decorations on page 143
- writing form on page 144
- 12" x 18" (30.5 x 45.5 cm) construction paper
- optional decorative items (buttons, feathers, beads, sequins, etc.)
- scissors and glue
- crayons or felt pens
- stapler

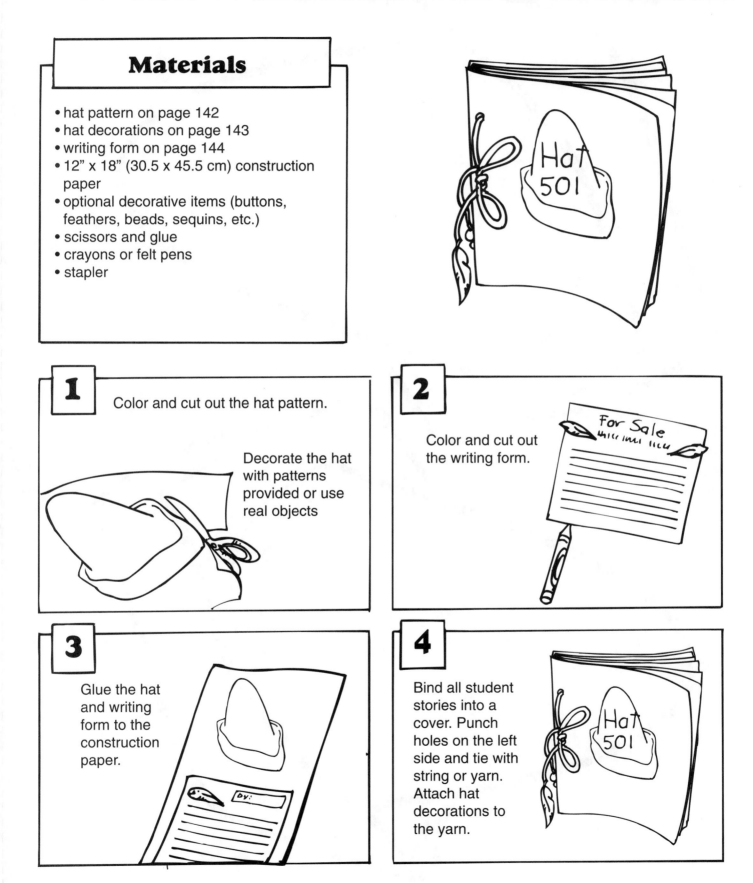

1 Color and cut out the hat pattern.

Decorate the hat with patterns provided or use real objects

2 Color and cut out the writing form.

3 Glue the hat and writing form to the construction paper.

4 Bind all student stories into a cover. Punch holes on the left side and tie with string or yarn. Attach hat decorations to the yarn.

Read a Book, Make a Book EMC 778

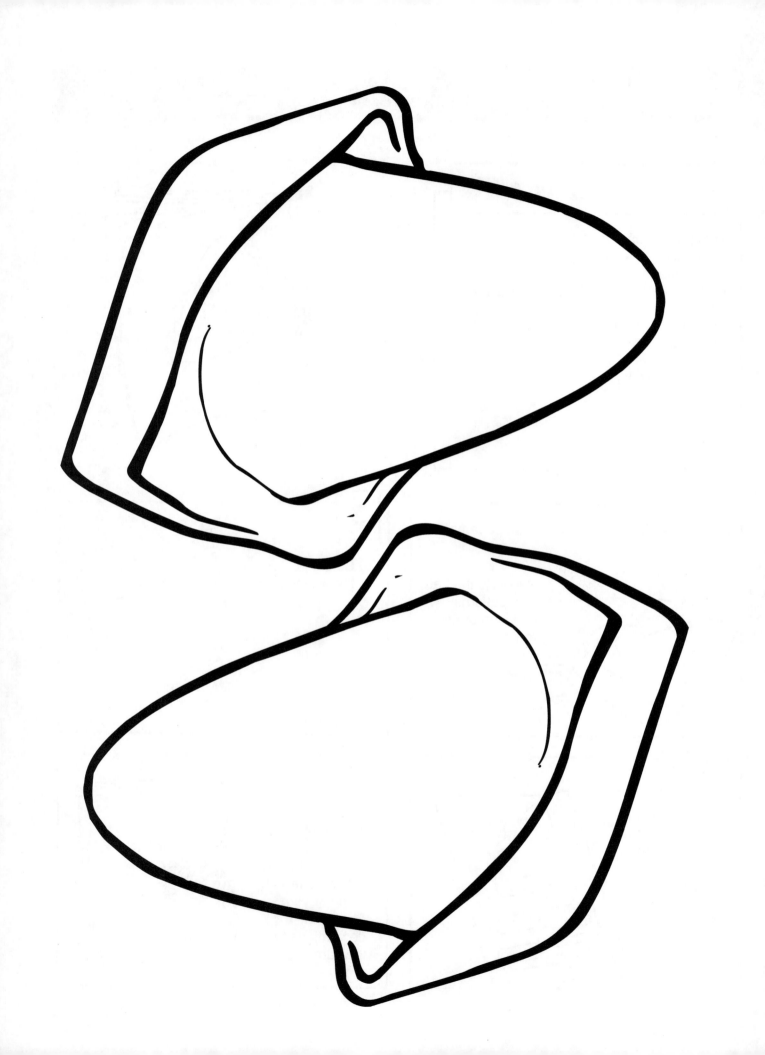

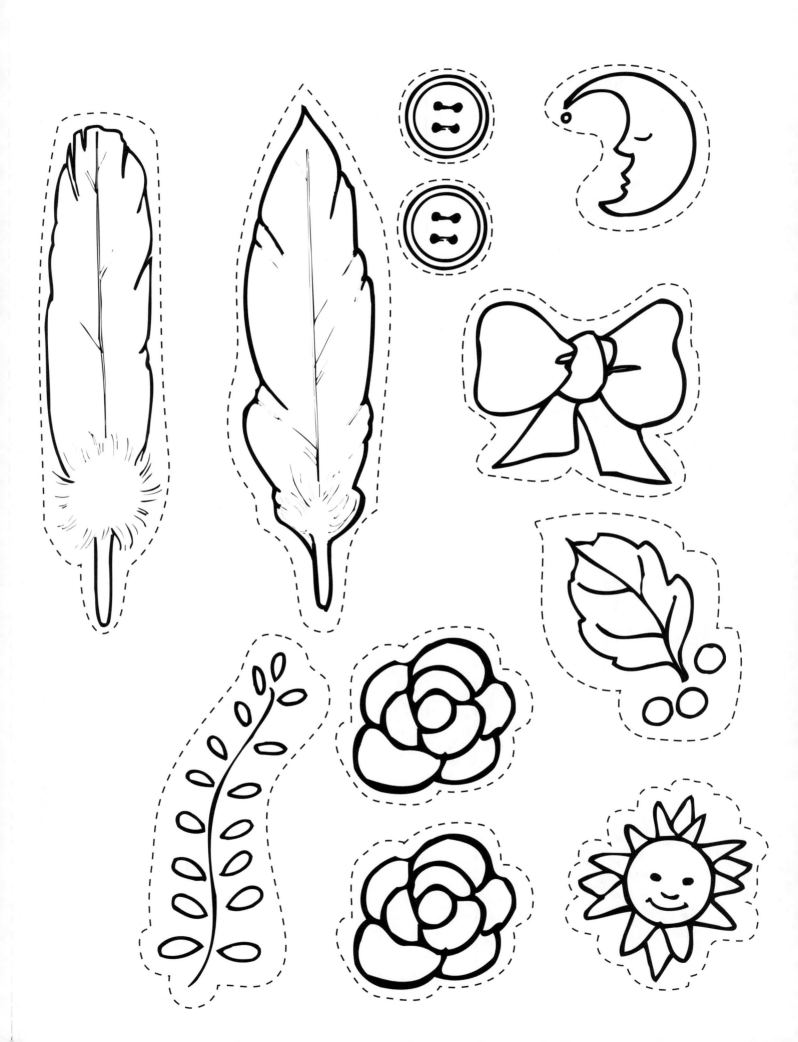

For Sale

The Fabulous, Fantastic Hat 501

One Potato

by Diana Pomeroy; Harcourt Brace, 1996

Book Project

After You Read

Provide real objects for students to count in sets of ten.

Now Write!

Students can choose fruit and vegetable patterns to color and paste in the spaces between the numeral and the number word. They then draw the correct number of the item.

One strawberry

    Two strawberries

        Three strawberries

        Four

Five strawberries

    Six strawberries

        Seven strawberries

      More

Jill Norris

Read a Book, Make a Book EMC 778

Make a Book...

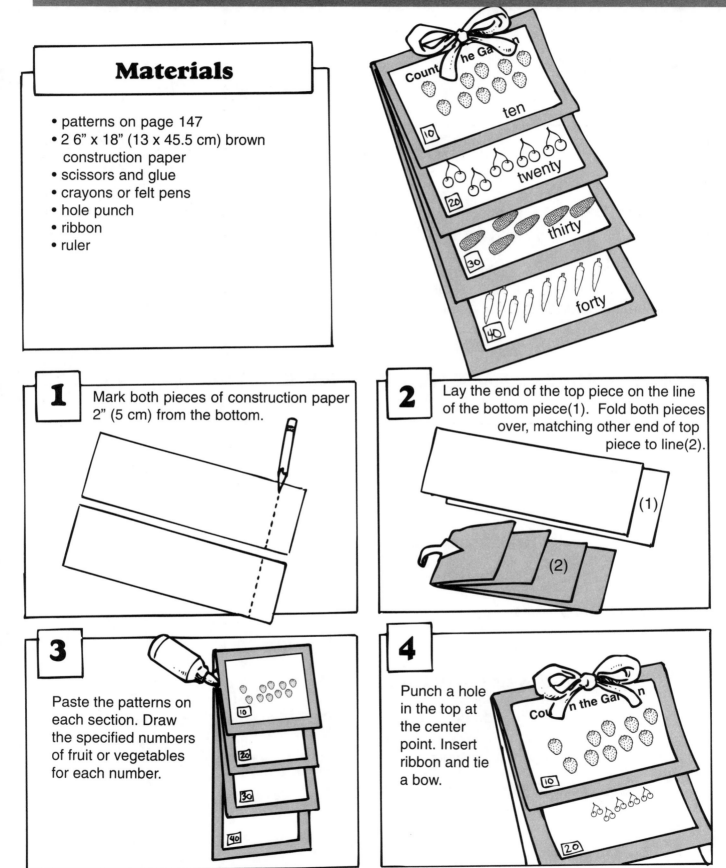

Materials

- patterns on page 147
- 2 6" x 18" (13 x 45.5 cm) brown construction paper
- scissors and glue
- crayons or felt pens
- hole punch
- ribbon
- ruler

1 Mark both pieces of construction paper 2" (5 cm) from the bottom.

2 Lay the end of the top piece on the line of the bottom piece(1). Fold both pieces over, matching other end of top piece to line(2).

(1)

(2)

3 Paste the patterns on each section. Draw the specified numbers of fruit or vegetables for each number.

4 Punch a hole in the top at the center point. Insert ribbon and tie a bow.

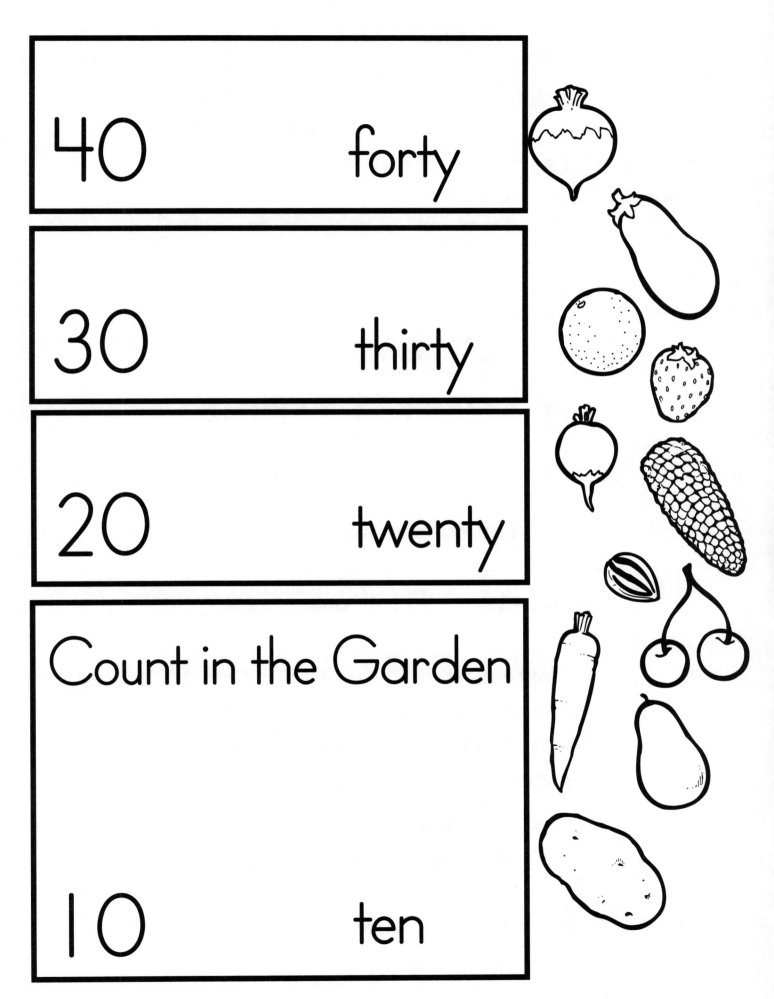

40   forty

30   thirty

20   twenty

Count in the Garden

10   ten

 Read a Book, Make a Book EMC 778

Fortunately

by Remy Charlip; Four Winds Press, 1964

Book Project

After You Read

Tell a Good News/Bad News story with your class.

- Have one person tell a good thing.
- A second person adds something that is bad.
- The third person adds another good thing.
  and so forth...

Continue in this pattern until all have had a chance to add something.

Now Write!

Write a "Fortunately" book following the style of Remy Charlip's book.

Fortunately	Unfortunately
I found a dime.	It was bedtime.
My bank will hold it.	Too full. It won't fit.
I'll use this cup.	Oh no! Mom washed up.
My dime survived.	My big brother arrived.

Sorry Bud, that's my dime.

Better luck to you next time.

Jill Norris

Make a Book...

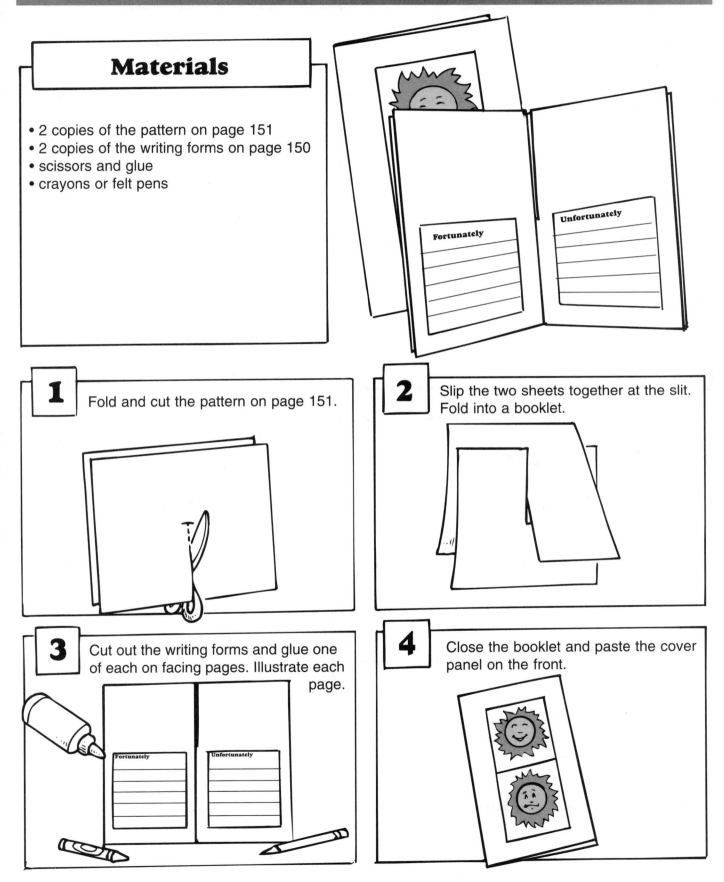

Materials

- 2 copies of the pattern on page 151
- 2 copies of the writing forms on page 150
- scissors and glue
- crayons or felt pens

Fortunately

Unfortunately

1 Fold and cut the pattern on page 151.

2 Slip the two sheets together at the slit. Fold into a booklet.

3 Cut out the writing forms and glue one of each on facing pages. Illustrate each page.

Fortunately   Unfortunately

4 Close the booklet and paste the cover panel on the front.

Fortunately

Unfortunately

fold ———————————————— cut

Read a Book, Make a Book EMC 778

Seven Chinese Brothers

by Margaret Mahy; Scholastic, 1990

Book Project

After You Read

1. Each brother in this story had a special talent or ability. Discuss the brothers and their special talents.

2. Then have students think about and identify at least one special talent that they have. Make a list of these abilities. Encourage the inclusion of character traits such as dependability, kindness, helpfulness, etc.

3. Talk about how the brothers worked together and compare this with the way your class works together to achieve a goal.

Now Write!

Younger students can write about each of the brothers and his special talent. Older students may want to write about themselves and classmates.

Do the job that you do best.

Leave the others to the rest.

Work together as a team.

You will soon achieve your dream.

Jill Norris

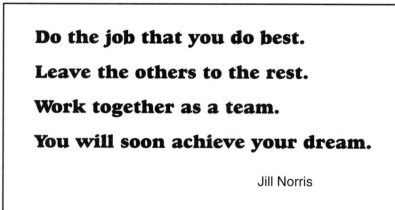

Make a Book...

Materials

- 2 copies of writing form on page 154
- 12" x 18" (30.5 x 45.5 cm) construction paper
- scissors and glue
- crayons and felt pens

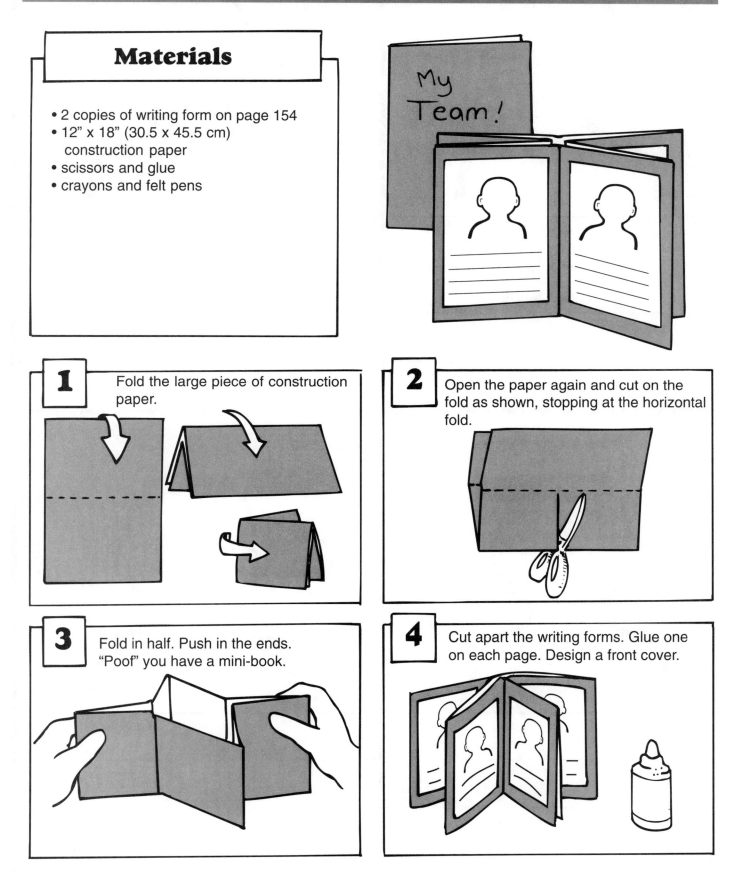

1 Fold the large piece of construction paper.

2 Open the paper again and cut on the fold as shown, stopping at the horizontal fold.

3 Fold in half. Push in the ends. "Poof" you have a mini-book.

4 Cut apart the writing forms. Glue one on each page. Design a front cover.

The Icky Bug Alphabet Book

by Jerry Pallotta; Charlesbridge Publishers, 1986

Book Project

After You Read

Jerry Pallotta's alphabet books are wonderful nonfiction references for making student books. It's fun to create books around a theme—a unit of study, a country, a holiday, etc.

Now Write!

You may want younger students to work in pairs, so that fewer pictures need to be drawn.

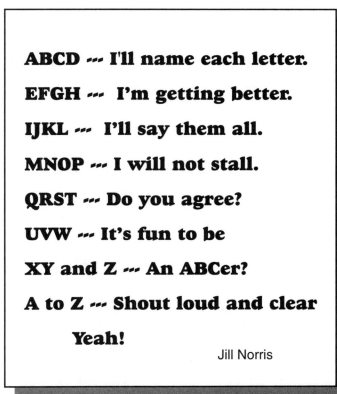

ABCD --- I'll name each letter.

EFGH --- I'm getting better.

IJKL --- I'll say them all.

MNOP --- I will not stall.

QRST --- Do you agree?

UVW --- It's fun to be

XY and Z --- An ABCer?

A to Z --- Shout loud and clear

     Yeah!

Jill Norris

Make a Book...

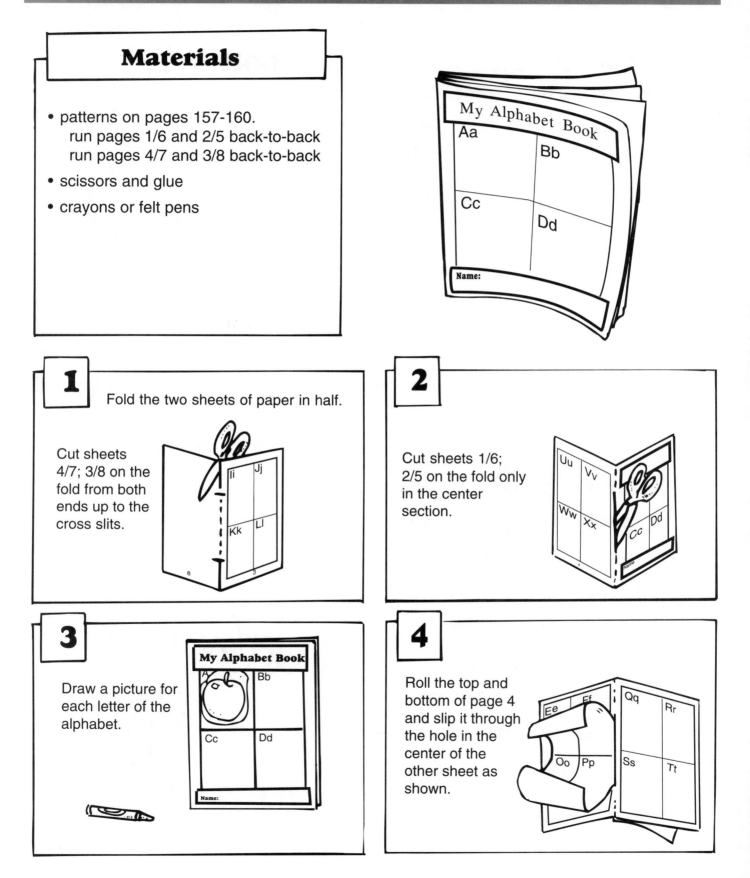

Materials

- patterns on pages 157-160.
  run pages 1/6 and 2/5 back-to-back
  run pages 4/7 and 3/8 back-to-back
- scissors and glue
- crayons or felt pens

My Alphabet Book
Aa
Bb
Cc
Dd
Name:

1

Fold the two sheets of paper in half.

Cut sheets 4/7; 3/8 on the fold from both ends up to the cross slits.

Ii Jj
Kk Ll

2

Cut sheets 1/6; 2/5 on the fold only in the center section.

Uu Vv
Ww Xx
Cc Dd

3

Draw a picture for each letter of the alphabet.

My Alphabet Book
A Bb
Cc Dd
Name:

4

Roll the top and bottom of page 4 and slip it through the hole in the center of the other sheet as shown.

Ee Ff
Oo Pp
Qq Rr
Ss Tt

Read a Book, Make a Book EMC 778

Uu

Ww

Vv

Xx

6

--- fold --- | --- cut --- | --- fold ---

Name:

Cc

Aa

Dd

Bb

My Alphabet Book

1

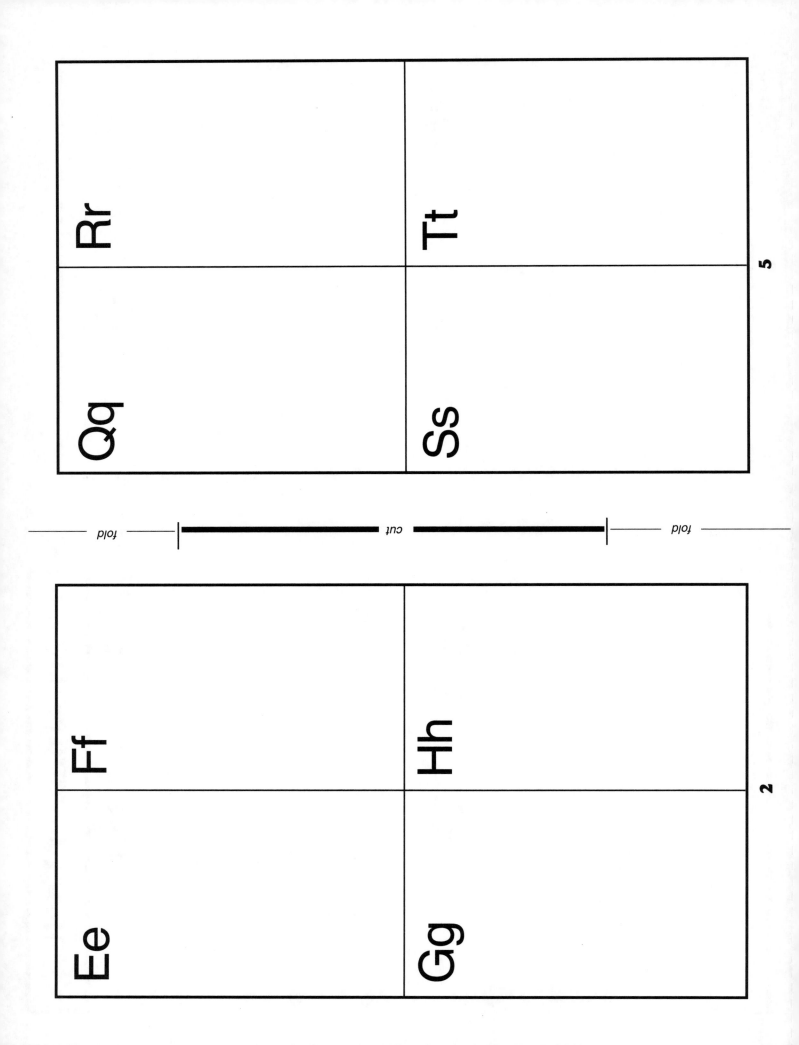

Rr

Qq

Tt

Ss

fold — cut — fold

Ff

Ee

Hh

Gg

Mm

Nn

Oo

Pp

Yy

Zz

ABCD --- I'll name each letter.
EFGH --- I'm getting better.
IJKL --- I'll say them all.
MNOP --- I will not stall.
QRST --- Do you agree?
UVW --- It's fun to be
XY and Z --- An ABCer?
A to Z --- Shout loud and clear
            Yeah!

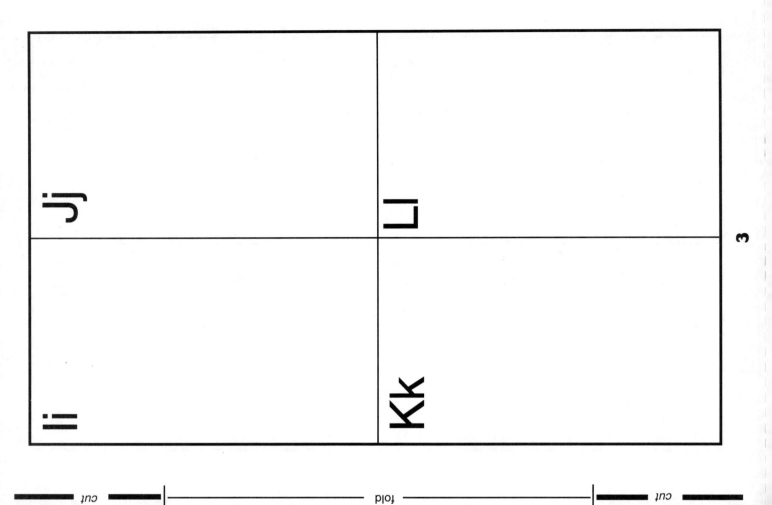

Jj

Ii

Ll

Kk

cut ———|— fold ———————|— cut